# GLOBAL CITIES A SHORT HISTORY

A SHORT HISTORY

# GLOBAL CITIES

*Greg Clark*

BROOKINGS INSTITUTION PRESS
*Washington, D.C.*

*Copyright © 2016*
THE BROOKINGS INSTITUTION
1775 Massachusetts Avenue, N.W., Washington, D.C. 20036
www.brookings.edu

The Brookings Institution is a private nonprofit organization devoted to research, education, and publication on important issues of domestic and foreign policy. Its principal purpose is to bring the highest quality independent research and analysis to bear on current and emerging policy problems. Interpretations or conclusions in Brookings publications should be understood to be solely those of the authors.

*Library of Congress Cataloging-in-Publication data are available.*

ISBN 978-0-8157-2891-7 (pbk : alk. paper)
ISBN 978-0-8157-2892-4 (ebook)

9 8 7 6 5 4 3 2 1

Typeset in Sabon

Composition by Westchester Publishing Services

# CONTENTS

# ACKNOWLEDGMENTS

I WAS DELIGHTED WHEN my colleagues at the Brookings Metropolitan Policy Program proposed the idea of this book. Writing *Global Cities* has been both a significant challenge and an honor. I am very grateful to colleagues at the Brookings Institution in Washington, D.C., who supported me and encouraged me in this endeavor, especially Alan Berube, Marek Gootman, Joe Parilla, and Elizabeth Patterson. I am also very grateful to colleagues at the Brookings Institution Press for the calm and professional manner in which they helped plan the text and its launch. My appreciation goes to Valentina Kalk, Carrie Engel, and Janet Walker.

I must also thank JPMorgan Chase, without whom this book would not have been possible. Its generous support to Brookings through the Global Cities Initiative has helped metropolitan leaders understand their global starting point and advance and grow their regional economies by strengthening international connections and competitiveness. Hopefully this book will provide an additional resource for their efforts.

Back in London, my "home team" of Dr. Tim Moonen, Emily Moir, and Jonathan Couturier aided considerably in assembling the case studies, refining the story, proofreading the manuscript, and telling me to keep going. Without their contributions, this book could not have been written.

The text benefited substantially from several reviews by knowledgeable individuals who were generous and supportive, and who also made multiple suggestions for improving the text, all of which I adopted. I am very grateful for their thoughtful contributions.

I must also record my personal thanks to those whose work is cited in this book. There is a large and substantial literature on global cities, globalization, urbanization, and trade, and this book has benefited greatly from the expert scholarly work of others.

Last, the driving motivation for accepting the invitation to prepare this book was my extensive working relationships with practitioners and scholars in more than 100 cities globally. My overarching desire was somehow to translate our rich conversations we enjoy into a text that would crystallize some of what we jointly know. To those friends, thank you.

*London, 2016*

# ONE NAVIGATING GLOBAL CITIES

A SHORT HISTORY OF global cities is hard to write because the history of global cities is a long one. But what a story it is!

From the founding of the great cities in antiquity, well before modern nation-states emerged, through to the rise of the digitally driven global cities of today, with their fresh livability equations and innovation ecosystems, the history of global cities is deeply entwined with the story of human civilization. In many ways, the current cycle of urbanization invites a fresh look at the primacy of cities that is observable in this history.

This short journey through the histories of global cities explores key aspects of the evolution of global cities in the past and the prospects for such cities in the future. (For clarity and consistency, the term *global city* rather than *world city* is used throughout the book.) It does not try to offer a new definition of global cities; the work is concerned with observed history rather than with theory. But I have sought to reflect on the assessments that others have made as part of that history. To that end, five key features that manifest over time in cities that develop roles beyond domestic markets warrant mention. These are:

1. cross-border trade through connectivity,
2. diverse and entrepreneurial populations,
3. innovation and influence over systems of exchange,
4. the discovery of new markets, products, and practices, and
5. geopolitical opportunity.

Through these features we can chart the evolution of globalizing cities in the interest of discovering their DNA, and allow the cities to tell their own stories as parts of one continuous history (box 1-1).

The expression *global cities* is of recent coinage, but the idea is not new, and this book goes back into history to find its origins. Today, three big phenomena are helping to focus interest and attention on global cities and their multiple functions.

First is the *rising number of global cities*. There is a new generation of globalizing cities today, and many more global cities exist than in previous cycles of globalization. Some studies identify more than 150 substantially globalized cities among more than 500 urban areas with a population in excess of 1 million people.[1] As regional and global economic integration increases, and as more cities achieve critical mass, the number of global cities is expected to increase every year. Not every city, of course, can become a global city, in either economic or

BOX 1-1.  **THE REVEALED INGREDIENTS OF GLOBAL CITIES**

- Trade and connectivity
- Diverse and entrepreneurial populations
- Innovation and influence
- Discovery of new markets, products, and practices
- Geopolitical opportunity

cultural character. But the number of cities whose economies are international in their orientation is sufficiently large that it makes sense to talk about globalization as driven by, and produced through, the activities of global cities.

Second is the phenomenon of *metropolitanization*, The twenty-first century is the "metropolitan century," and in many respects the story of global cities is now one of larger urban agglomerations, or what are called metropolitan areas (metros for short). Growing cities have spilled over their old boundaries and accidentally have become complex functional areas that compose a single economic unit, even as older jurisdictional boundaries are maintained. Over the last century many cities have been on this trajectory of metropolitan dispersal, but *metropolitanization* now also denotes a way in which cities can absorb population and economic growth within several connected population centres and pursue reurbanization and densification as they seek to become more managed metropolises. With metropolitanization and reurbanization at the fore, it is expected that the world's population growth and settlement pattern will eventually level off at more than 80 percent urban by 2100. Barring other disruptors, the pattern of cities globally and the infrastructure platforms that support them will be largely set for the next 100 years that follow. So the cities that rise to prominence in the coming years and find their way to global influence and relevance have an opportunity to sustain advantages for a long time to come.

And third, *global economic dynamics are changing.* Since 2008 a major shift has taken place as the global economy reorganizes after the banking crisis and worldwide recession. The world's center of gravity is rapidly moving east and south. This creates new market opportunities for cities that were on the edge of things, and forces cities in more established parts of the world to fight to remain relevant and influential. As prosperity becomes more evenly shared across (if not within) nations, the mobility and reach of the new global middle classes underwrite a much bigger reservoir of consumer demand. The extension of prosperity also means that the economic and spatial balance of nations is being reshaped and is allowing more medium-sized and second-tier cities to acquire and develop complementary trade specializations.

These three factors—more global cities, the new century of metros, and changing global economic dynamics—make the present a timely moment to review the short history of global cities.

This history is one of diverse groups of cities globalizing in distinctive ways, where "globalizing" describes the process of cities' economies becoming highly international and global in character. Some of them, like the mature global cities of the past quarter century—New York, Tokyo, Paris, London—became centers for corporate headquarters and decisionmaking, providing advanced finance and expert professional services to multiple sectors, firms, and nations. But many of the global cities of earlier eras were not of that kind. Historically, there have been many ways for cities to engage globally, with trade and discovery playing fundamental roles. Today and in the future, it seems certain there will be even more imperatives and ways for cities of different types and in different contexts to "go global." Chapter 2 reviews the links between and among cities, trade, and connectivity over time.

Global cities have emerged, thrived, and declined in distinct phases. These phases, which generally seem to occur in waves, are enabled not only by geographic discovery and the opening of new trade routes. They are also driven by scientific discovery and invention, by technological developments, and by geopolitical changes that bring specific kingdoms, dynasties, empires, or colonies to the fore. More recent waves since the nineteenth century have been associated with the development of ports, canals, aviation, automation, advanced manufacturing, creative and cultural offerings, the rise of transnational corporations, and the growth of global urbanization itself. The different infrastructures, innovations, and traded sectors that have powered these waves mean that diverse pathways are available to cities becoming global. Since about 1980, waves of globalization have been distinguished by the worldwide expansion of capital markets and financial services, and by the deregulation and global spread of business media and information services. But it makes little sense to think of global cities as only financial or media centers, or indeed to think of such cities historically solely as imperial capitals or port cities. The discussion in chapters 3 and 4 takes up why and how cities globalized over time, what made some cities global cities and others not, and what factors allowed certain cities to sustain global roles for longer periods of time while others declined.

The two most recent waves of globalization of cities since the 1980s have also seen the development of corresponding bodies of academic work to define, theorize, and measure what is meant by "global cities." This emerging science of global cities is being pursued in different places through an increasingly connected global community of scholars and analysts that includes at least the Chinese Academy of Sciences in Beijing, the Mori Memorial Foundation in Tokyo, the Brookings Institution and the World Bank in Washington, D.C., the Organization for Economic Cooperation and Development in Paris, UN-Habitat in Nairobi, the wider United Nations and the Ford Foundation in New York, the LSE Cities Group in London, the McKinsey Global Institute in New York, the World Economic Forum in Geneva, United Cities and Local Governments in Barcelona, and the African Centre for Cities in Cape Town. In addition to this work are more than 200 indexes, benchmark reports, and global reviews of cities that are produced by a wide range of organizations, including the Globalization and World Cities Group, the *Financial Times*, the *Economist*, Jones Lang LaSalle, Mercer, Mastercard, PricewaterhouseCoopers, the Chicago Council on Global Affairs, and many more. Chapter 5 reviews the evolution of thinking about and observation of global cities and how these bodies of thought have developed and changed. The discussion considers global city analysis today and the different ways in which the global system of cities is interpreted.

The current cycle of globalization, which emerged from the 2008–09 recession, is characterized by new distinctive and differentiated types of global cities and new alternative paths to becoming one. This proliferation of pathways is a result of the increased mobility of people and capital, the globalization of multiple functions and business sectors, and the emergence of new technologies and demographics. We are already familiar with the established global cities, such as New York, Hong Kong, London, Paris, Singapore, and Tokyo, those cities that led the globalization wave of the 1980s to 2008 and are now developing new additional niches of specialization. But the growth of such new specializations provides opportunities for other cities also to host leading functions in globally integrated value chains. The rapid development of newly advancing economies and large nations, such as China, India, Brazil, Indonesia, and Korea, has given rise to a new set of *emerging global cities*, or major cities with a growing global influence. Meanwhile the newly internationalizing sectors of life sciences and medicine, digital and screen industries, clean tech and renewable energy, traded urban services, and other advanced industries are fueling a new generation of globalizing cities, such as Brisbane, Nanjing, Oslo, San Diego, Santiago de Chile, Stockholm, and Tel Aviv.

Chapter 6 considers the different types of global cities extant today and the different trajectories cities have followed in moving from one type to another or developing hybrid forms. The cities in each group combine national and regional roles with cross-border and global roles, and require specific competences to play those roles capably.

As such they often tend to possess similar assets and to share broadly similar imperatives. Of keen interest to observers is how these cities can continue their global path in the future. A number of common factors become evident: global orientation, business climate, talent and technology, connectivity, livability, the ability to manage growth through land use, housing, and infrastructure investment, and governance arrangements that are durable across metropolitan areas and can deliver negotiated solutions with nation-states.

Recent history has also shown that global cities produce their own tensions and frictions. These tensions are manifest not only within the city itself but also in its relationships with the nation-state and with wider economic geographies. On the one hand, globalizing cities can create extraordinary value for business sectors, workers, and enterprises, and they contribute amply to public finances through tax payments. On the other hand, globalizing cities pose substantial growth management challenges that result from their pace and scale of growth. Mature global cities also endure strained relations with the broader provincial, state, or national economy in which they participate. They are often perceived as emitting *centripetal forces* that attract skills, investment, resources, and businesses from the wider economy in which they are located, weakening the performance of other cities in the process. This drain of business and skills can lead to political animosity and encourage national or state-level governments to perceive their primary priority as one of constraining the growth of the global city and attending to the needs of those cities and regions outside it. Despite evidence of the way global cities also often act as *centrifugal forces* to push activities and opportunities to other cities that are well connected with them, complementary strategies have proved stubbornly difficult to advance in many cases. These debates and conflicts are set to become a major part of the agenda for global cities in the future.

Leadership, therefore, is critical to the future of global cities. City leadership comes from many sources, not just municipal or metropolitan governments. Its task is to address both the challenges that face global cities and the imperatives raised by the relationships between globalizing cities and their broader national or state economies and polities. Chapter 7 looks at the key challenges and leadership imperatives faced by globalizing cities and reviews the different models of leadership that are operant. It also explores leadership coalitions, the roles of civic, institutional, and business leaders, the critical dynamics between local and national governments, and the question of how to organize metro areas. The role of learning and networking between cities is also explored. This chapter looks forward to the near future and imagines what the future system of global cities on some continents might look like. In this way, the patterns of the historical past can be viewed in the context of future drivers and disruptors, to the extent that speculation about these is possible.

This short history is illuminated throughout by different examples of global cities around the world and across the ages. I refer frequently to globalizing cities and to global cities. This is because the globalization of cities occurs through processes that are never absolute or complete. The book does not seek to offer a comprehensive account that covers all the cities and city types that have ever been active in globalization. Rather, its writ is limited: it simply seeks to illustrate the rich variety of stories and messages that emerge from the way cities have engaged with global opportunities.

# TWO ORIGINS: TRADE AND CONNECTIVITY

THE ROOTS OF THE global city can be found in the trading city. Historical links between cities and trade have left a deep imprint on the way global commercial patterns have evolved. This chapter looks at how trade and connectivity are the underlying drivers for cities to become outward-looking and globally oriented.

The urge to trade, and to develop cities that can facilitate the exchange of goods, ideas, capital, and people, lies at the heart of much of what is thought of as modern capitalism. It is within cities that boat-building, cartography, navigation, currencies, insurance, stock exchanges, and banking were developed to support trade. In the modern era, global cities support and host global stock exchanges, financial institutions, professional services, advanced and creative industries, and technological innovations. But trade facilitated by and in cities also predates capitalism by several millennia.

In the ancient world it was between cities that the great trade routes for silk, spice, sugar, and tea developed, and it was trade that spurred city growth and the civilizing tendencies that cosmopolitan cities produced. Trade brought immigrants and merchants to port cities and commercial centers, creating the human mix that spurred cultural and knowledge exchanges and encouraged innovation. Arguably, trade has historically been the biggest external stimulus for societies to change and develop.[1] It is responsible for many of the breakthroughs in technology, banking and insurance, fashion, and creativity—though without doubt it is also inextricably connected to the experience of slavery, exploitation, and human suffering.

THE EVOLUTION OF TRADING CITIES   For more than three millennia, cities have operated as junction boxes for flows of goods, capital, information, and people. Among different and changing political and theological systems, cities have proved to be the units best suited to the spatial concentration of industries, and this concentration in turn has driven industrial specialization, labor market pooling, information sharing, and productivity.[2]

As trading systems mature, it is common for merchants to build up a series of trade settlements and form a network of dispersed commercial hubs that mediate and broker relationships between different cultures. Historically, cities have often become places where people of different origins clustered on a semipermanent basis out of mutual interest, in this way bringing into being the first examples of cosmopolitan cultural diversity. The networks that cities form have generated interactions between previously insulated cultures and regions, aided by technological advances and new modes of accumulating capital. Flexible and multifunctional trading cities have also come to exert influence over other, more monofunctional places, creating local relations of dependence and hierarchy.

Table 2-1 summarizes the history of cities and trade through ten trade routes, along which many cities became externally oriented and significantly globalized. The table identifies some of the key moments in the evolution of the relationships between cities and trade and lists the important innovations and externalities of each cycle. Of course, many other trade routes existed besides these, not least the overland routes between Russia and China, the trade systems in Africa and Mesoamerica, and the maritime routes that flourished at the height of the British Empire.

Nearly 10,000 years ago several of the earliest cities developed trading specializations and internal divisions of labor, and their connections to trade routes were vital to their rise or fall. Çatalhöyük, a large Neolithic settlement in modern-day Turkey, and Jericho, in modern-day Palestine and also dating from the Neolithic period, were among the first trading cities; over time, they achieved remarkable advances in technology and organizational culture. Çatalhöyük traded in obsidian, dates, and shells from across Turkey and the Middle East, while Jericho's location next to a ford on the Jordan River allowed it to become a trade center for salt, sulfur, and asphalt with cities throughout the region.[3]

Within a few thousand years of the first city civilizations, advanced and complex trade networks had become

**TABLE 2-1. TEN GREAT TRADE ROUTES IN HISTORY**

| MAIN TIME PERIOD | TRADE ROUTE | PROMINENT CITIES INVOLVED | INNOVATIONS PRODUCED | NEGATIVE IMPACTS |
|---|---|---|---|---|
| 1000 BC–AD 400 | Mediterranean | Alexandria, Antioch, Athens, Carthage, Constantinople, Massila (Marseille), Rome, Tangier | Ship-building, spread of literacy, alphabet, Greek philosophy, Roman road network | Conquest and enslavement |
| 400 BC–AD 1600s | Silk Roads | Alexandria, Baghdad, Bagram, Constantinople, Ctesiphon, Damascus, Dongguan, Guangzhou, Hangzhou, Herat, Kabul | Trade caravans, paper, gunpowder, compass, algebra, medicine, astronomy, irrigation, printing, banking and coinage | The Black Death, Hunnic and Mongol invasions, religious violence |
| AD 1050–1500 | Mediterranean | Barcelona, Florence, Genoa, Marseille, Naples, Pisa, Venice | Financial innovation, spread of luxury goods, long-term suppression of piracy | Democratic impulses displaced by dynastic rule |
| AD 1250–1550 | Northwestern Europe (Hanseatic League) | Antwerp, Bruges, Hamburg, London, Lubeck, Novgorod, Riga, Stockholm | Commercial organization, ship-building, banking, administration | Restrictive trade monopolies |

| | | | | |
|---|---|---|---|---|
| AD 1500–1750 | African circumnavigation and Indian Ocean | Colombo, Dares Salaam, Lisbon, Luanda, Mumbai | Cartography, improvements in navigation, advances in natural history | Slavery, colonial conquest, monopolistic practices, internal division |
| AD 1500–1800 | Atlantic Triangle | Amsterdam, Havana, Kingstown, Lisbon, London, Madrid, Nassau, New York, Paris, Rio de Janeiro, Rotterdam, Salvador, São Paulo | Improvements in navigation, ship-building, mercantilism, early capitalism, spread of Enlightenment ideals, property rights, capital markets, telegraph, canals | Slavery, conquest, and economic division, social dislocation in Africa, piracy |
| AD 1600–1800 | Southeast Asia to Latin America | Bangkok, Batavia, Calcutta, Guangzhou, Melacca, Mexico City, Nagasaki, Penang, Saigon, Singapore | Silk and spice routes; silver, porcelain tea | Divergence between Asia and Europe, colonization |
| AD 1850–1940 | Pacific Rim | Guangzhou, Los Angeles, Macau, Osaka, Tokyo | Silver exports, state modernization | Indentured labor; tension in U.S.-Japan relations |

*(continued)*

TABLE 2-1. Continued

| MAIN TIME PERIOD | TRADE ROUTE | PROMINENT CITIES INVOLVED | INNOVATIONS PRODUCED | NEGATIVE IMPACTS |
|---|---|---|---|---|
| AD 1945–1970s | North America–Europe | Chicago, Detroit, Hamburg, Munich, Toronto | Global consumer goods, shared economic and regulatory frameworks, information-based logistics | Narrow economic specialization, sprawl, environmental pollution |
| AD 1980s–present | Asia-Pacific | Bangalore, Guangzhou, Hong Kong, Mumbai, Singapore, Shanghai, Shenzhen, Sydney | Production and IT innovations, infrastructure development, poverty reduction | Environmental pollution, resource damage, integration of rural migrants |

established, enabled by designed infrastructure. By the third millennium BC, an urban hierarchy of more than twenty city-states had formed in Mesopotamia, loosely organized around the central city of Uruk. Ur was one of the "second cities," benefiting from its proximity to the Euphrates and the Persian Gulf entrance and linked by a canal to cities across Mesopotamia, the Persian Gulf, and ultimately even the Indus valley. It was one of the first cities to plug into long-distance trade routes, importing copper and ivory from the East. Offices were even constructed along the riverbank to supervise trade. The stability and prosperity afforded by trade created a platform for the city to nurture a number of mathematical breakthroughs in architecture and astronomy. The technologies of the time meant that cities at the farthest ends of long transport links did not trade directly with each other, and divisions of labor were not common as they are now. Nevertheless, cities at this time were fundamentally dependent on their connectivity: Ur's success was cut short only when the Euphrates later changed its course, around the second century BC, which denied Ur the necessary water for irrigation and a waterway for trade.

The propensity of cities to trade grew in part as a response to the militarization of early kingdoms and empires, and sea-based transport in particular gradually emerged as highly important. As early as 1300 BC the enterprise of politically autonomous Phoenician cities such as Tyre and Sidon saw them operate in the interstices between feuding Mediterranean empires, specializing in trade exports such as glass, textiles, dye, and tin. The Phoenicians were pioneers of an early form of merchant capitalism and were among the first to develop a maritime

FIGURE 2-1.  PHOENICIAN TRADE NETWORK

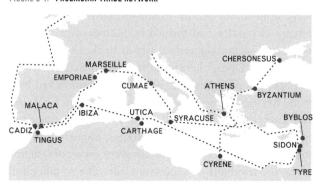

regional city network (figure 2-1).[4] Originally from the Levant, this merchant and maritime civilization founded settlements across the whole Mediterranean. Carthage was one of its leading outposts, founded in 814 BC in modern-day Tunisia. At its height, it was the strategic core of a chain of cities that spread along the Spanish, French, Sicilian, and North African coasts, with trading conducted as far away as Cornwall, in southwest England.

Other important breakthroughs and innovations in the execution of trade were made early on in the history of globalization. One important example came during the First Persian Empire. Under Darius the Great (ruled 522–486 BC), a silver and gold coinage was established and a regulated tax system created that was adapted to the economic needs and capacity of each regional province, or *satrapy*. This was one of the first of many examples of long-distance trade driving financial innovations around currency exchange, asset management, and insurance. Infrastructure was key to the exchange of ceramics

FIGURE 2-2. THE ROYAL ROAD—LONGEST ROAD NETWORK IN HISTORY ON COMPLETION CA. 500 BC

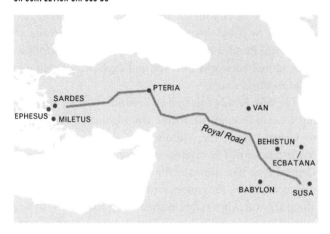

and other commodities across the empire—a 1,600-mile highway included the famous Royal Road from Susa to Sardis and on to Persepolis and Ephesus (figure 2-2). This road linked preexisting roads into a network, and horseback couriers working in relays could reach the remotest areas within two weeks. This unprecedented degree of connectivity allowed imperial inspectors to tour the empire and report back on local affairs. A system of customs duties, tolls, and tariffs on trade was a major source of imperial revenue, facilitating the investment in city development and further transport. A 45-meter-wide canal was also dug to link the Red Sea to the Nile.

The system of reliable and rapid communication had a lasting influence on future leaders and diplomats, who recognized the importance of connectivity to the projection of central authority over a large land mass.[5] Although the purposes of infrastructure were initially military and governmental, the availability of a road system stimulated a new wave of commerce and knowledge exchange, led especially by Babylonian, Jewish, and Phoenician traders.[6] The Royal Road was an early sign of what was to follow: truly global networks of trade and exchange, facilitated by horses and roads.

The Silk Roads emerged in around 400 BC, connecting a chain of cities stretching from China's Pacific coast to Central Asia, the Middle East, and eventually the Mediterranean. The expansion of nomadic Scythians into Central Asia had dramatically increased the role of long-distance trade in the region, with merchants paying tariffs along the way. City-states located along the routes thrived by trading with each other and by offering refuge and services to passing trade caravans. These cities were much more than stopover points. Many became what today might be called logistical and trade hubs, between which goods, ideas, people, and services flowed. More than just a network of trade routes linking the East and the West, the Silk Roads were really, in the words of the historian Christopher Beckwith, "the entire political-economic-cultural system of Central Eurasia."[7]

The network of Silk Roads expanded dramatically when Alexander the Great conquered much of Central Asia in the fourth century BC (figure 2-3). His successor kingdoms built the infrastructure and security necessary to expand trade routes eastward. He also founded a string of cities bearing his name along the way—Alexandria, Herat, Kandahar, and Bagram, among others—all of which became brokerage points and safe havens along the routes linking the Mediterranean to India. These early global

FIGURE 2-3.　MAP OF CITIES ALONG THE SILK ROADS, 300 BC–AD 100

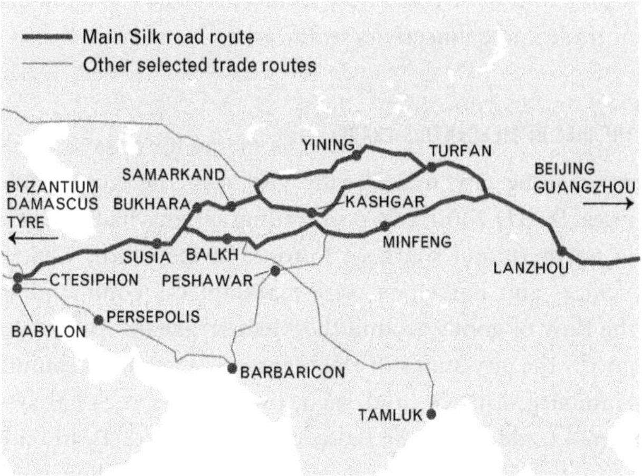

cities were very culturally diverse, with strong mixes of Persian, Greek, Indian, and even Chinese cultures. As Chinese dynasties pushed westward, more routes were built to carry silk, spices, precious stones and ores, food, and ideas, linking urban centers from Kaifeng and Guangzhou to Ctesiphon and Alexandria.

From Alexander's conquests until the present day, the networks and cities of the Silk Roads have remained. The rise and fall of different cities was sparked by war, disease, religious tumult, and climate change. Constantinople, Karachi, Sindh, Baghdad, Kabul, Antioch, Kashgar, and Dunhuang all enjoyed their moment in the sun as leaders and merchants adopted different tactics in a volatile geopolitical arena.[8] Although competitor trade routes, new markets, and new production processes diminished the importance of the Silk Roads in the second millennium

AD, the impulse toward globalization is an undimmed legacy, and these roads now form a template for a new era of trade and connectivity in Eurasia.[9]

**THE RISE OF MERCANTILE TRADE**    The model for today's modern trading city was already visible in the late Middle Ages. By AD 1300, two port trading systems had emerged in northern and southern Europe. In the south, Genoa, Venice, and Barcelona were marketplaces commanding the flow of goods around the Mediterranean. And in the north, the city-states of the Hanseatic League, including Hamburg, Lübeck, and Riga, organized a regional system of trade across the Baltic countries (box 2-1). In both cases the networked cities took advantage of their position between competing jurisdictions to create their own legal instruments that could sustain lucrative trading operations, without the need to undertake territorial expansion or impose large-scale taxation.

In the absence of strong sovereign states, peer pressure and mutual self-interest encouraged city traders in Europe to create private solutions to enforce contracts and keep distant merchants honest. Recent research has also shown that, in a world that was politically fragmented, city governments became competitive in their quest to attract international trade by continually adjusting their logistics and their legal, commercial, and financial institutions to suit the needs of traders.[10] Even when merchants did not dominate the city government (as in Antwerp and Venice), the ambition to become a big international market incentivized city leaders to welcome foreign trade and adapt local institutions. Competition between trading cities

BOX 2-1. THE HANSEATIC LEAGUE

After the fall of the Roman Empire, most northern European cities were inward-looking, isolated, and feudal. Long-distance trade and more outward-looking economies slowly reemerged, thanks to the determination of merchants in league with city-states.

In the thirteenth century, at a time of commercial change in Europe, a network of cities known as the Hanseatic League was established to facilitate trade across the Baltic. Merchants no longer had to move from city to city but instead could direct trade from urban headquarters, working through intermediaries. As merchants became powerful local political actors, they became more involved in city leadership. The Hanseatic League was founded as a collective of merchants defending their interests across multiple cities. It eventually evolved into an association that cooperated to defend the members' trade routes and privileges.

The league was based around the coastal cities between the Baltic and North Sea, with the city of Lübeck initially its key member. An axis was formed that eventually stretched from London via Bruges and Bergen to Stockholm, Gdansk, Riga, and Novogorod in Russia. It was instrumental in reconnecting northern Europe to long-distance trade.

The cities of the league developed many assets familiar in today's global cities. Specialization and diversification took place, including in ship-building, fishing, furs, cloth, salt, credit, and infrastructure. As league members were de facto city leaders, they worked hard to maintain the rule of law and predictable trade rules across their network. Among their major achievements were ensuring quality control, harmonizing the value of weights, measures, prices, and sharing market intelligence to ensure a transparent trading environment up until the 1500s.

The league's leaders strongly resisted attempts to cut them off. They maintained a fleet of trading vessels and when necessary could mobilize an army of up to 300,000 men to defend their trade routes. They also negotiated fiercely with feudal overlords to expand their markets and protect their trading rights. Even though the league had no official legal status, it had many of the attributes found in today's global cities: outward-looking leadership, commercial interest groups, and advocacy with higher authorities. It was only the rise of territorial nation-states that would prove the league's undoing, but traces of its influence remain visible today, as does the success of many of the cities in its network.

## HANSEATIC LEAGUE TRADE ROUTES

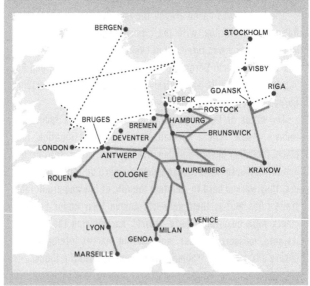

appears to have been a longer-standing feature of the economy than was previously recognized.

City trade networks were not confined to Europe in the early stages of globalization. In Southeast Asia, before the arrival of the Portuguese and the Dutch from the sixteenth century, an elaborate interregional trading network formed around Melacca and Canton (Guangzhou), involving a number of port gateways in modern India and southern China. Melacca, for example, was as important to the region as Venice was to Europe.[11] Port cities and entrepôts—intermediary centers of trade and transshipment—formed a vibrant network sustained by Arab, Indian, Chinese, and Japanese traders. Then as now, infrastructure and tax systems were at the heart of cities' attractiveness to trade. Trade towns flourished and hosted multiethnic populations from across Asia and even Europe. In Asia as in Europe, the late Middle Ages saw cities prosper as formal or informal city-states. Many, such as Bandar Abbas, Banten, and Surat, operated largely independently of imperial powers and coercive trading companies.

At least some of the cities that globalized through trade in earlier globalization waves survived the changes and the predatory regimes of later centuries and are now seen to be forging new international orientations. Other cities that were once major transportation and business centers went into relative decline, including Antwerp and Seville. In both cases, the silting up of their rivers was fundamental to enabling other cities (Amsterdam, Cadiz) to become more competitive. In Seville's case, other factors thought to have contributed to its decline included the high share of foreign ownership of the city's assets. The same concerns are frequently raised about cities today.

THE RISE OF THE NATION-STATE    From the seventeenth century on, the trading power of cities and city-states was partly stifled by the emerging nation-states, which were able to generate administrative, regulatory, and fiscal leverage over their territories. Former city-states typically came under the control of powerful European armies and empires. Nations directed this new wave of globalization through their colonial ventures, often creating new cities from scratch to tap lucrative trade routes; two examples here are Calcutta and Penang. In the West in particular, nation-states gradually fostered productive economies of scale and home market effects, which meant that industries with high transport costs tended to grow within nations rather than across nations.

But the ascendancy of the nation-state did not entirely inhibit the trading networks of cities. Between Europe and North America, economic globalization between 1600 and 1900 saw growing industrialization and trade capabilities cluster around modern cities, and these cities became the engines driving the economies of national trade processes.

By the eighteenth century, commercial relationships were well established between western European cities such as Bristol, Glasgow, Liverpool, and Dublin and merchants operating in colonies across the Americas. Amsterdam, Lisbon, London, and Antwerp were the foremost centers of the diamond trade.[12] American coastal cities also developed sophisticated trading relationships, exporting rum, timber, furs, tobacco, wheat, and meats across the Atlantic, and this export trade fueled the growth of Boston, Salem, Charleston, and Philadelphia, among many other coastal cities. The Atlantic trade began to fundamentally change social and political structures in these cities and surrounding rural areas and triggered competition for new markets, and for new goods and services to sell.[13]

Elsewhere, dense maritime city trade networks stabilized in regions such as Southeast Asia, involving Bangkok, Penang, Canton, Singapore, Saigon, and Manila. These cities were a frontier for colonization by global players such as the East India Company, but they also operated with some degree of independence in their own commercial zone. Cities in the Ottoman Empire also played active trading roles. Izmir was profoundly integrated into European financial circuits, exporting silk, cotton, and wool through Marseille and other ports. Like many others, it gained a cosmopolitan population attracted by the opportunities of European trade.

Transport connections improved markedly in the nineteenth century, enabling a surge in trade and investment worldwide. Indeed, compared to all other time periods in the history of globalization, "the mixture of quantitative take-off and qualitative change [in the nineteenth century] . . . was unprecedented."[14] The rate of increase in world trade went from a historical average of 1 percent per year to around 4 percent between 1820 and 1870. The nineteenth century was the century of mass energy production, long-term capital investment, and monetized economies. World expos took place for the first time, showcasing global trade and industry. Entrepreneurial immigrant trade networks became an increasingly important presence in such cities as Hong Kong, London, and Shanghai, especially around the entrepôts where global trade was managed.[15] Many of the historical changes were enabled by colonization, which also meant very rapid technology transfer, especially of steamships, railways, trams, and, later, motor vehicles. By 1903 the American monthly magazine *The World To-Day* was highlighting the step change for cities' connectivity: "In the old world, cities were separated by the distance a horse could travel in a day. In the new world, the great cities are separated by the distance a railway train can go in twenty-four hours, with large secondary cities about twelve hours' ride between."[16]

The first half of the twentieth century saw a slowdown in the global rate of urbanization. This coincided with the rise of communism and fascism, the two world wars and their attendant destruction, and a significant drop in global trade. The ratio of world trade to global GDP returned to its pre–World War I level only in 1973. National economies looked to trade mainly within the sphere of their own national or colonial systems.[17] Cross-border sourcing took place locally, such as between U.S. and Canadian cities in the auto industry or between European cities in machinery.[18] Innovation, scale, and specialization in North American and European cities continued to create cost advantages that favored the retention of manufacturing rather than relocation to cities in the global south.

## MULTINATIONAL COMPANIES AND A NEW CYCLE OF GLOBAL TRADE
In the 1960s and 1970s the control of nation-states over patterns of international trade began to loosen with the onset of deregulation. Companies in advanced economies found strong incentives to internationalize and escape national constraints. Modern multinational

firms came to play a critical role beyond their national or imperial origins as a result of technological and institutional changes that supported the internationalization of production, trade, and investment. The revolution in information and communications technology made it possible to coordinate trade complexity at a distance, and cities such as Singapore sought to position themselves as servicing and distribution platforms for multinational firms. These firms drove new patterns of specialization, whereby cities tended to grow into one of the following:

- sites of standardized low-cost production,
- hubs of research, development, design, and administration, or
- proficient transport intermediaries through containerization or aviation.

The number of multinational businesses grew tenfold between 1970 and 2005. By the 1980s these firms accounted for three quarters of world trade outside the socialist bloc.[19] Cities and corporations became the key players within complex global production or supply chain networks, enabled by the internationalization of currencies, exchange rate trading, and the growth of the Eurodollar market. The rise of transnational corporations saw different cities come to play distinct roles in a new international division of labor, and many cities were able to take advantage of opportunities to reverse the threats that globalization had posed to their manufacturing and back-office economies. What transpired is that transnational corporations *needed* cities.

**THE NEW GLOBAL CYCLES**     Since the 1980s, political and economic changes have accelerated "the integration of world trade and disintegration of production," in the words of the economist Robert C. Feenstra.[20] Political transformation and the rise of democracy in Latin America, eastern Europe, and Asia saw many of these regions' larger cities direct their manufacturing and residence functions toward trade, exchange, and consumption roles. In East Asia this trend has been especially pronounced. Distributions of traders in key centers such as Hong Kong, Singapore, and Shanghai have promoted economic integration across the region, with coastal cities in the vanguard of a new cycle of global trade. An urban maritime corridor now stretches from Vladivostok to Singapore, characterized by a gradual convergence in legal systems and business practices.[21] This pattern of continental trading systems within an integrating global system is mirrored elsewhere, from northern Europe to Central America.

**SUMMARY**     In the current cycle since 2008, the extent to which a city's globalness correlates with its dependence on foreign trade may be less obvious than in the past. Cities that engage in a significant amount of foreign trade are strongly immersed in international markets and tend to experience other international-level dynamics, such as the move from trade in products to trade in value-added services, the international migration of skilled and unskilled labor, growth of the visitor economy, and cross-border capital flows. Trade is a trigger function for other forms of internationalization in an urban or metropolitan area economy.

This journey through some of the key moments in the relationship between cities and trade is followed in the next chapter by a more detailed review of the particular cities that played a part in this history, and of the other factors that have shaped cities' propensity and appetite to become global.

# THREE THE HISTORY OF GLOBAL CITIES I: ANCIENT CITIES

HOW DID A CRITICAL mass of cities operating in globally traded sectors arise? What light can global cities of times past shed on the likely character and duration of future global cities?

History shows that cities have tended to embrace international opportunities in waves and cycles. Cities rarely break out into international and global activity by themselves. They participate in collective movements or networks to take advantage of new conditions, and often their demise or withdrawal from a global orientation is also experienced jointly with other cities as circumstances change, affecting many at once. Of course, cycles of globalization are by no means uniform or linear. There is no fluid line of descent from ancient global cities and globalization processes to twenty-first-century cities. But there are clear patterns observable throughout history, and often the impact of one cycle is to set in train the winners and losers of the next cycle.

In the premodern, preindustrial age, cities became global in successive waves. These waves were synchronized with the occurrence of a number of critical enablers. Trade and connectivity, the subject of the previous chapter, formed one such enabler. This chapter highlights in addition the role of four others:

- entrepreneurial populations,
- innovation and influence,
- discovery of new markets, products, and practices, and
- geopolitical opportunity.

**THE FIRST WAVES**  It is hard to know when and where the first wave of global and globalizing cities really began, for globalization had precursors in the distant past and has been under way for several millennia.[1] The world's first great market-driven cities were established more than 4,000 years ago, in the Early Bronze Age, and their rich history is only now beginning to be understood. An urban revolution was taking place, with most residents of what is today southern Iraq living in cities, and this process of urbanization was accompanied by trade on a new scale.

Farther east the cities of Mohenjo-daro and Harappa, in modern-day Pakistan along the Indus River valley, were among the first cities with diversified economies and societies. They were located on trade routes that specialized in gemstones and spanned the whole of Central Asia.

These cities formed the epicenter of a vast trade network based on a common cultural and linguistic community, and built infrastructure to provide good standards of living for residents. With their deep-rooted cultures and external orientation, they exhibited many of the hallmarks of what are now considered to be global cities.

In the first and second millennium BC, numerous other cities came to display incipient global instincts and linkages. The centers of early Mesopotamian civilization, such as Akkad, Babylon, and Ninevah, were among the first to build major infrastructure systems and gain independent city rulers. Bactra, in modern-day Afghanistan, was a highly mature trade and export management center. Persepolis and Pasargadae were the nucleus of a pioneering road network that allowed the speedy flow of messages across Asia. As these cities built long-distance links, the spread of ideas, concepts, and influences across cultures began to intensify for the first time.

One important lesson to be drawn from the early waves of urbanization and the long-distance activities of cities is that prized assets and luxury possessions have often been drivers of interconnection and collaboration. As China began to expand its horizons, the trade in horses, silk, bamboo, rice, and wine was vigorous and often used in diplomacy to guarantee peace between empires and cities. Silk even became an international currency. Safe and efficient transport between cities on Bactrian camels was highly sought after. Within a few hundred years, the world had been effectively shrunk by the growing sophistication of the trade network. As Peter Frankopan notes, "We think of globalization as a uniquely modern phenomenon; yet 2,000 years ago, it was a fact of life, one that presented opportunities, created problems and prompted technological advance."[2]

The rise and fall of empires often fundamentally shaped the opportunities cities had to build their trading economies. Rulers and dynasties often flip-flopped in their approach to city-based merchants, sometimes reducing taxes and offering free rein to operate, at other times introducing severe restrictions and disincentives to trade. This means that for nearly all cities that globalized prior to AD 1000, the story of their globalization was one of repeated interruptions, occasional catastrophic decline, and a slow return to glory. In some cases, but by no means most, cities expressed a core ethos of tolerance, openness, and commercial aptitude whenever their rulers provided stability and let these values flourish.

## Eurasia and Africa

Connectivity with the Eurasian trade system allowed Indian cities to thrive just as Rome was reaching its zenith. After climate change and invasions by rural Aryan tribes had seen the original Indus urban settlements fade, an urban renewal gathered pace, really taking off in the third century BC. In the aftermath of Alexander the Great's conquests, the Mauryan Kingdoms (322–185 BC) became highly productive administrative, military, and trade outposts that afforded a safe trading environment, made heavy investment in roads, and conducted a well-coordinated export business of diamonds, cotton, and spices to Rome. Taxila, northwest of today's Islamabad, stood out as a major gateway, while the imperial city Pataliputra, adjacent to today's Patna and near the Ganges river, flourished. Tamralipti also emerged as a major port serving trade with Sri Lanka and East Asia. Even after the collapse of the kingdoms, coastal trade with the Persian Gulf, East Africa, and East Asia continued, feeding the growth of the port of Barygaza, located at the mouth of the Narmada river on the west coast of India, which traded with imperial Rome.

The first European city to develop networks akin to those of a modern global city was Rome (box 3-1). Its empire came to consist of a federation of cities—stretching from Spain and Scotland in the west to the Euphrates river in the east—each of which had a territory attached. Rome provided the administration, the stability, the monetary regime, and the tax structure for cities to thrive amid a huge spike in population mobility and mercantile activity.[3] By the mid-Roman era, most contemporaneous historians perceived the world to have been globalized. Polybius in his *Histories* remarked that "from this point onwards history becomes an organic whole: the affairs of Italy and Africa are connected with those of Asia and of Greece, and all events bear a relationship and contribute to a single end."[4] Among the lasting features of this wave of globalization of trading cities was a much larger and more diverse trading of goods across continents. This trade fueled a new commercial zone in the Indian Ocean and direct trade with India. The Roman urban network also helped spread religion, and cities in the Roman system later became centers of Christian authority. This era was perhaps the first time that one city's power and influence became the fundamental driver of intercontinental trade.

While the rise and fall of Rome as a global city is well documented, others have resumed global roles whenever the geopolitical opportunity has presented itself.

BOX 3-1. THE ORIGINAL GLOBAL CITIES: ATHENS, ALEXANDRIA, ROME

ATHENS. The external orientation of ancient Athens was achieved and sustained through networks and influence. The city's mineral wealth and strategic location made it an early center for manufacture and trade, not least of pottery (exported) and grain (imported). Under ruler Peisistratus, the city rapidly expanded Athenian commerce and improved trade relations in the region, setting the stage for the city-state's prosperity. At no point was Athens the largest city or the one best connected to long-distance trade routes. But its leadership created deep alliances with a network of up to 250 Mediterranean cities forming the Delian League, which exchanged goods, people, and ideas in a relatively free market. Foreigners always played a prominent role in the city's industry and trade, and up to 10 percent of Athens's population was thought to be foreign.

Like New York City today, Athens projected influence through its ideas and innovations. Grand public buildings, including temples and emporiums, gave Athens iconic status and appeal for visitors and intellectuals. The city set a benchmark for civilization and rational inquiry, in opposition to rural and "alien" barbarism. Its political culture of assemblies and democracy was replicated in Rome and farther afield. Athenian philosophy, tragedies, and comedies would also become the template for much European and Middle Eastern thought and literature.

ALEXANDRIA. Founded by Alexander the Great, Alexandria grew as a major Mediterranean grain producer, with links to North Africa, Europe, and Asia. The city grew phenomenally through feeding first the Greek cities and later the Roman Empire, and by passing on exotic wares from the Silk Roads. It had grown to 300,000 people by the Roman imperial period, probably second only to Constantinople. Alexandria's trade position made it one of the most multicultural cities of its day. It was home to Greeks, Macedonians, Jews, Persians, Egyptians, Syrians, Arabs, and Italians. In the third century BC, the number of foreign traders in the city was so high that problems were reported in exchanging currency. The entrepreneurs it attracted promulgated new ideas, and it became the center for scientific research for the entire Mediterranean, with probably the largest library of its time. Even when it was absorbed into the Roman Empire, it remained a jewel in the region, acting as one of Rome's gateways to the east.

ROME. Unlike Alexandria, Rome did not open to the world by selling its surplus. The city began life as an unpromising regional backwater, and Roman generals, senators, and emperors later expanded it through conquest—first of Italy, of Carthage and Gaul, then of the grain basket of Egypt, and finally of the rich Silk Road gateways in the eastern Mediterranean. Conquest provided cheap food, new goods, and a surge in Romans' purchasing power. Demand for slaves, spices, silks, and other exotic items soared. Rome's population grew as the young and ambitious flocked there for political, bureaucratic, or military advancement. At its height, the city had over 200 trades and a uniquely wide division of labor. The city became a sophisticated command center for administrative and commercial networks that spanned the entire Mediterranean basin.

Much like cities today, Rome needed sound communications and good infrastructure to sustain its might. It laid down a huge road network, nurtured professional leadership, and coordinated the movement of an extraordinary number of troops and goods. Ultimately the costs of maintaining these supply networks would lead to fatal overstretch. The city proved incapable of stemming waves of invasion, and it became cut off from its supply networks, which triggered the collapse of the Western Roman Empire.

BOX 3-2. GLOBAL CITIES OF THE CHINESE DYNASTIES

From the third century BC to the 1400s, Chinese cities were among the wealthiest and largest in the world. Their place in a large, rich, and progressively unified territory and their strategic location as gateways to the Silk Roads and Pacific trade meant that well into the Ming dynasty (1368–1644), they dwarfed their counterparts in Europe.

| MAJOR CITY | DYNASTY UNDER WHICH IT WAS DOMINANT | KEY CHARACTERISTICS |
|---|---|---|
| *Chang'an* | Han, 202–8 BC | Rise of a money economy, publicly owned industries, innovations in mathematics, astronomy |
| *Luyoang* | Han, Tang, and Zhou, 1st–2nd centuries AD | Repeal of government monopolies, invention of paper and the seismograph |
| *Kaifeng* | Song, 960–1127 | Investment in joint stock companies and sailing vessels, merchant guilds. |
| *Beijing* | Ming, Qing, 1421–1644 | Privatization, wage labor, investment in ventures, trade in silver and weapons |
| *Guangzhou* | Song, Ming, Qing, 11th–14th, 18th–19th centuries | Maritime gateway city, limited trade licenses |

CHANG'AN (XI'AN). In China's north, Chang'an (now Xi'an) was founded around 200 BC and was one of the earliest dynastic capitals. Like its successors, it grew as the seat of power in a highly centralized system, where production and regional trade were tightly controlled. Its leaders developed a sophisticated statistical and commercial intelligence apparatus. Its status and that of Luyoang, which succeeded it as capital, were boosted by the emergence of long-distance trade and what would become the Silk Roads.

## FOREIGN NETWORKS AND RELATIONS IN SOUTHEAST ASIA DURING THE MING DYNASTY

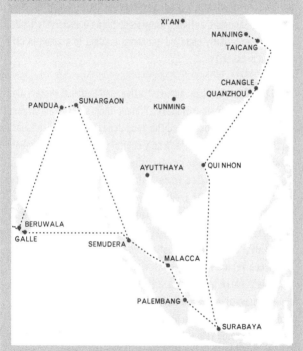

KAIFENG. The rise of the Song dynasty led to the establishment of Kaifeng as the new capital. At its height in the tenth and eleventh centuries AD, it was home to over a million people. Located at the

Continued

junction of the Yellow River and 30,000 miles of riverways and canals, Kaifeng was one of the most outward-looking cities of its time. It also sat at the heart of a region of 120 million people connected by trade and a mature system of cities. Successive emperors and administrators gradually relaxed central control over trade and economic activity. They made China a decisively trade-oriented, externally engaged economy, leading to a boom in city size and prosperity.

HANGZHOU. China's urban, administrative, and political system also proved adaptable to setbacks. Violent incursions from steppe warriors in the 1100s forced the Song dynasty south to the more fertile Yangzte River Delta. A new capital was formed, Hangzhou. It too became one of the largest cities of its time. Not only was it plugged in to land-based trade, notably of celadon ware pottery, the most beautiful yet produced, it also benefited from connections to Guangzhou and a maritime trade largely dominated by Arab merchants. Marco Polo was reportedly impressed by its size and wealth, and by the sophistication of Chinese technology, at a time when Venice was home to fewer than 50,000 people.

China's early globalizing cities waned from the fourteenth century onward. Mongol invasions and the Black Death led to a period of retrenchment. The Ming dynasty, in reaction to what it perceived as foreign (Mongol) incursion, progressively wound down long-distance maritime trade, and a period of isolationism began. China's cities, while still impressive, largely turned their back on the world from the 1500s, with trade licences often revoked, until the European colonial powers came visiting in the nineteenth century.

Istanbul is one city that has experienced many cycles of global exchange over the last two millennia because of its unique strategic location as a bridge between Europe and Asia. Formerly named Byzantium, the city was transformed by Emperor Constantine in the fourth century AD and renamed Constantinople because it was close to Rome's economic and political interests in the eastern empire. Roman leaders needed an open city located close to Rome's supply market along the Silk Roads, across the Black Sea, through rich Anatolia, and into the wheat-producing areas of the Nile. As a result, Constantinople assumed command-and-control functions and drew ambitious Roman citizens and traders from around the world.

As a cultural melting pot, Constantinople facilitated the spread of Christianity across the Roman Empire. Despite the collapse of the Western Roman Empire, Constantinople later resumed its role as a vibrant trade hub in the eighth and ninth centuries. Under a tight system of state control over factories, workshops, wages, and tariffs, the city processed trade from Russia, India, China, and Africa, with merchants attracted by its gold and silk commodities. It transported goods to and from Venice, Pisa, Genoa, and all over Europe, and at one point is said to have been home to 60,000 Italians.[5] Much later, under the Ottomans, Constantinople became Istanbul. Its leaders grasped the new opportunities of European trade and actively invited the intelligentsia of the Islamic world. While Istanbul's influence has waxed and waned, its strategic position has repeatedly proved an asset to outward-looking leaders and has created an enduring appeal to immigrant entrepreneurs and innovators.

Many of the later waves of global cities unfolded according to Sir Walter Raleigh's maxim: "He who controls the seas of the world controls the trade of the world; he who controls the trade, controls the world."[6] Competition between cities was a major feature throughout the premodern period. For example, in the ninth and tenth centuries rivalries between the Islamic dynasties (the Abbasids and Fatimids) saw bitter struggles between their respective capitals, Cairo and Baghdad. Despite political instability Cairo successfully established trade relationships with the Byzantine Empire and southern Europe at Baghdad's expense (box 3-3). The ability to secure trade routes and to be open to ideas and knowledge saw cities like Cairo draw scholars and intellectuals from across the Muslim world, while Europe at this time was largely immune to cosmopolitan influence.

### Mesoamerica

Eurasia and North Africa were far from alone in hosting cities with advanced capabilities and trading impulses. Mesoamerican cities in the pre-Columbus era had large regional supply systems, but high transport costs often inhibited the long-term expansion of trade links and cooperation. Teotihuacan, close to today's Mexico City, had reached its height around the beginning of the European Christian era, growing into a planned metropolis of 100,000 people. Trade was mostly on foot, exchanging urban manufactured goods such as obsidian and stone tools for rural agricultural surpluses.

In Mesoamerica, and especially during the Aztec Empire in the fifteenth century, a large group of professional

If Rome became a global city through conquest, Baghdad emerged as one because of it. It was one of many cities established in the eighth century after the lightning takeover of Central Asia by Islamic forces. Located on a strategic site close to the fertile and trade-friendly Tigris and Euphrates rivers, for a long time Baghdad remained one of the richest and largest cities of the premodern world. Incredibly, it exceeded 1 million inhabitants at its peak in the tenth century.

MAP OF ANCIENT BAGHDAD

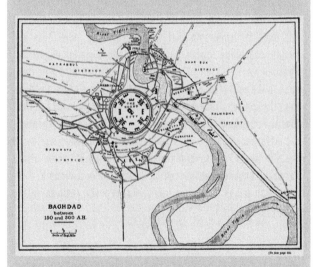

© William Muir, 1883.

Continued

By the late 900s, the Eurasian trade routes largely sat within a unified Abbasid caliphate, stretching from the Atlantic to the gates of China. A single and open market with political stability and military security, united by common currencies, rules, and customs, drove an explosion in trade, with Baghdad at its center. It was made the political capital of the caliphate and was designed as a showcase of Islamic power and wealth. The caliphs ensured the city drew in goods, tribute, people, and taxes.

Baghdad's prodigious wealth, and openness to tradesmen and visitors also allowed it to become the center of global ideas and innovation. Spectacular advances in medicine, mathematics, optics, astronomy, and philosophy emerged thanks to a theological and political leadership that was receptive to new ideas and people, especially Jewish, Zoroastrian, and Christian minorities. Baghdad was everything European kingdoms were not at the time: open to the world, adaptable, and thirsty for knowledge. However, the city began to face competition as Islam's dominant intellectual and commercial center from Cairo and Alexandria. Theological differences and military turmoil split the Islamic world and the Silk Roads into several fragments, choking off many of the networks Baghdad had thrived on. It was finally overrun by Central Asian tribes and never recovered its lofty position on the global stage.

merchants called *pochteca* formed an integrated association of upwardly mobile traders who engaged in the dangerous long-distance intercity trade of lightweight, high-value goods. They oversaw how the marketplace operated and provided banking, retail, and wholesale services.

Across the broader region, many great cities emerged, such as Tikal, Copan, and Palenque in the Mayan Empire, Chan Chan in the Chimu Empire, and Cuzco under the Incas. Many were high-altitude cities that did not rely on river or maritime traffic and engaged only in limited organized long-distance trade. Although in some cases the road networks were more advanced and facilitated a wider basin of trade, trade between cities was mainly in ideas and techniques, including crop cultivation, writing, and religion. Ultimately, however, these cities were unable to sustain their regional trading functions. Although many factors and explanations exist, it is clear that environmental damage, resource scarcity, social divisions, and the European invasion all played a part in their demise.[7]

THE EUROPEAN COMMERCIAL ECONOMY WAVE: AD 1150–1350   A new wave of cities developing international roles took place in the eleventh and twelfth centuries AD as part of what is sometimes called the "commercial revolution." As population and urbanization grew, a two-pronged system of cities emerged: the lucrative trade in the Baltic Sea and the North Sea of Europe was gathering pace in some, while many Italian city-states were becoming prosperous through shipping, commerce, and banking. This was a time when many systems of rule and governance coexisted. As cities grew, they became independent or semiautonomous entities with their own military capability. This wave of globalization was also characterized by a powerful merchant class that dominated the market economy and had an active role in city leadership.

Italian cities took advantage of geopolitical opportunity during the Crusades to expand their trading and banking services for the military campaigns. Venice in particular gained privileges in the Byzantine Empire and extended relations with the pope. Italian cities also benefited from a population influx of artisans and traders that resulted from agricultural innovations that created surplus. Nobles also migrated to cities to become manufacturers or financiers. Together with the merchants, they discovered a vast panoply of new and improved practices, including those having to do with accounting, financial instruments, commercial law, and business management. Specialization in the silk industry followed, not just in Venice but also in Florence and Lucca. Initially involving importing raw silk and designs, specialization later entailed the vertical integration of silk production and eventually exporting to eastern markets, where Aleppo, Alexandria, and Cairo were the major trade entrepôts. With Italian success came influence. By the late 1200s, Florence and Genoa were minting gold coins, and Florence's own currency became dominant in European commercial and financial markets.

This wave marked the first time that so many regions and religions had come into sustained contact. Janet Abu-Lughod has identified eight regional circuits in operation, stretching from northwestern Europe all the way to modern-day Malaysia and Philippines.[8] It was also a time in which cities achieved great cultural, artistic, and intellectual advances, spawning both trade and knowledge exchange. The circuits Abu-Lughod describes thus fostered interregional contact through cultural gateway cities such as Venice in the West and Melacca in the East. In between, the geopolitical opportunity for peace after the thirteenth century Mongol invasions was also a catalyst for ports and caravan cities in the Middle East to develop and globalize. One example was Tabriz, in modern-day Iran, which attracted a large number of European merchants and was described as the most cosmopolitan city in the world in the thirteenth century. It specialized in gold and silk cloth weaving and in trade in precious stones. Five hundred years later the city was still noted for its independent merchant class.[9]

The Black Death devastated many of the leading cities in this wave, but the advanced network of the Hanseatic League and the globalizing cities in southern Europe endured into the fifteenth century, brought together by a shared desire to conduct free trade. This wave is thus often seen as vital to the later spread and success of modern capitalism.

THE POST-COLUMBUS WAVE: AD 1500–1650     Beginning in around 1500, cities that had globalized in the previous wave began experiencing multiple and long-lasting setbacks. Agriculture was earning diminishing returns, and religious warfare gripped many cities. Italian and Iberian cities began to experience deindustrialization, uncompetitive wages, and loss of market share to cities in the East. A shift in favor of northern European cities began to take place.

Globalization had taken on new characteristics, with new roles for cities in a system where sovereign states were stamping their authority. Advances in map-making and ship-building helped improve communications and reduce transaction costs for cities. One change was in the nature of consumption. A new class of consumers appeared with a shared goal to signal position and status, driving major growth in production and retail sectors.[10] Gradually a much better connectivity emerged, characterized by an enlarged and integrated global market, new notions of a single world, and a sense of cosmopolitan identity, even though the system at this time was very much a hub-and-spoke model.

Northern European cities profited the most from this wave of globalization. At this point the beginnings of what became known as the "great divergence" between Europe and Asia appeared. Many arguments have been put forward to explain it. One factor was that merchants and bankers in (northern) European cities were able to protect their investments by legal means and to separate their capital from personal risk, which was not possible in Asian cities. A higher pace of urban growth, greater self-government for cities, and a strong trade focus in urban public policy have all also been suggested as key factors explaining the divergence.[11]

Another major factor was the rise of colonialism and the slave trade (figure 3-1). The city of Mbanza Kongo in modern-day Angola, located south of the Congo River, was one of many to become an important center for the sale and transport of slaves to South America, as well as the export of salt, copper, iron, ivory, and dyewood, in return for imports of luxury clothes and weapons. Interaction with Lisbon saw the city's rulers come to promote Catholicism and literacy. African-controlled commercial networks in the sixteenth century included Luanda and Kabasa. The longer-term trade development of these cities was halted by a worsening business climate and internal instability. Meanwhile, on the other side of the Atlantic,

FIGURE 3-1.  **SELECTED CITIES PARTICIPATING IN THE SLAVE TRADE, AD 1500–1650**

Salvador, Brazil had emerged as a major destination for slaves. Under the direction of an entrepreneurial elite the city became a major sugar and cacao exporter and processed a vast number of slaves to work on plantations. The city, however, became too narrowly specialized, and when the sugar economy declined in favor of gold and coffee, Salvador lost much of its influence to Rio de Janeiro.[12]

European cities are often described as the globalizing cities of this era, but Islamic conquests were also enabling a new group of cities to go global. From the early 1500s, northern Indian cities in particular were brought into a vast Muslim sphere of influence under the Mughal Empire. The unification of commercial practices, common customs, and beliefs allowed cities such as Delhi to become tightly integrated into Eurasian trade routes, especially for the export of textiles. Ahmedabad and Agra also thrived, aided by factory investment from the English East India Company, and, along with Delhi, reached a peak population of 400,000 people. Meanwhile Surat, nearly 200 miles north of Mumbai, became possibly the world's largest port, home to 150,000 people and at one point the richest city in India. The dividend of trade created a highly intricate division of labor, with manufacturing and artisan crafts feeding city interdependence. Vijayanagar was also one of the major religious and trade centers of Hindu India. Connected with ports in China, South Africa, and Burma, among others, it amazed foreigners with its wealth. Many assessments place these Indian cities' output at least on a par with leading European centers of the time.[13]

Antwerp and Amsterdam stand out as the two foremost global cities in continental Europe during this wave of globalization. Antwerp rose to prominence by cannily exploiting its gateway location at the heart of a rapidly expanding Hapsburg Empire. The fall of Constantinople in 1453 had weakened Venice and Genoa, and the Scheldt river made the city a gateway to navigable inland waterways reaching far into western Europe. When nearby Bruges' own port silted up, Antwerp's merchants made incremental gains in the wool and fabric trade, and Portuguese spices from the East Indies started passing through the port. By the mid-fifteenth century Antwerp had become a preferred trading hub between the Baltic, the North Sea, northern Italy, France, and the Holy Roman Empire. A few decades later the city's stock exchange and banking sector had become the largest in Europe.

Antwerp benefited from geopolitical advantage when it was absorbed into the Spanish Hapsburg Empire. This gave the city privileged access to a large unified market, and it became an entry point for silver and other precious goods shipped from Spanish American possessions. At its height, 40 percent of the world's trade was channeled through Antwerp. It was Europe's truly global city, with an ambitious and enlightened merchant class. The phenomenal wealth generated saw urbanization in the region reach 30 percent. The city's population peaked at 100,000 by the 1560s, but then the city suffered from Spanish insistence that Atlantic trade go through Seville—a way of diverting wealth to Spain. Entanglement in the Dutch revolt and religious conflicts saw the city sacked and repeatedly besieged. While it retained a merchant ethos, it never recovered its mantle as a global city, although its port is today resurgent.[14]

Amsterdam took over the mantle from Antwerp and Genoa as Europe's major commercial city during the 1600s, and it developed many of the technologies that underpin today's global cities. The overthrow of the Spanish elite, which had hampered the interests of powerful local merchants, granted more freedom to Dutch traders. Soon after, the blockade of Spanish Antwerp triggered a flight of capital and talented entrepreneurs to Amsterdam.

The Protestant city became prized for its safe port, political stability, and access to inland waterways. It maximized its appeal by guaranteeing equal protection to all merchants, wherever they came from, while developing standardized institutional norms. A relaxed attitude toward interest-bearing loans spurred the development of modern finance in Amsterdam, including maritime insurance, making the city both the logistical hub and the trade financier of Europe.

The establishment of the Dutch East India Company and a powerful navy helped Amsterdam secure control over trade routes and outposts as far away as Japan, Indonesia, India, and the Americas. The city's shipbuilders pioneered new materials and produced cheap cargo vessels, considerably lowering transport costs. Amsterdam gained sufficient leverage over supply chains to wage price wars, prioritizing volumes over margins to eliminate weak competition and secure a monopoly over pepper, tea, and sugar imports. But the impact of European wars and the rise of British naval supremacy in the eighteenth century meant that London eventually took Amsterdam's mantle. However, much of the know-how and assets acquired during Amsterdam's era of supremacy remain relevant today.

THE MERCANTILIST WAVE: AD 1650–1760    The next wave of globalization took place in the seventeenth and early eighteenth centuries with the expansion of European fiscal-military states in a mercantilist system. Two features were especially distinctive about this wave. First was the expansion of slavery, the trade in forcibly enslaved human beings. Cities such as Bristol, Buenos Aires, Charleston, Lagos, Liverpool, and New York participated actively in the slave trade. Lagos, for example, became a major international port by the mid-eighteenth century and became subject to British intervention.[15]

The second distinctive feature was the rise of finance and financial services as the management, borrowing, and investment of money began to shape cities more than previously. This wave is also notable for the rise in pre-industrial manufacturing, early forms of democratization in cities, and a growing economic divergence between Europe and Asia.

Despite the rise of great global centers in the West, such as London (box 3-4), other regions also became more globally oriented. At the height of the Mughal Empire in the 1650s, northern India was home to some of the largest cities and probably the most cosmopolitan, housing Persian, Turkic, Chinese, and Indian cultures. Southern Indian cities also created a mature trade network that benefited from vast local markets and a booming maritime trade along the Indian Ocean. However, from the 1700s onward foreign invasion and colonization would reshape India's urban geography and disrupt the potential of its globally oriented cities.

SUMMARY   This snapshot of premodern waves of globalizing cities highlights that the fortunes of externally oriented cities were never static, and that global networks of cities in times past were subject to very familiar forces to do with traded sectors, disruptive innovation, political and civil disorder, and climate changes. Figure 3-2 presents an indicative timeline of twenty cities that participated in these waves, highlighting the synchronicity with which

London has always been a trading center. The city lies on the Thames River estuary opposite the mouth of the Rhine, which places it ideally for trade with Europe. By the sixteenth century Richard Gresham, supplier of tapestries to Henry VIII's Palace at Hampton Court, had decided that London should have a purpose-built center for trade, along the lines of the Bourse in Antwerp. His son Thomas offered to build the City of London its own bourse at his own expense, if the City would provide the land. The Exchange survived until the Great Fire of London destroyed it in 1666, when it was rebuilt as the Royal Exchange. The number of merchants and traders operating at the Exchange spurred the creation of stock prices and commodities trading. Local coffee houses became an

THE ROYAL EXCHANGE IN 1810

extension of the trading floor of the Royal Exchange in the early eighteenth century, and these activities were eventually consolidated into the renamed Stock Exchange in the 1770s.

London was also one of the first global cities to specialize in the insurance market. Demand to insure expensive ships and cargoes grew, and the development of accurate shipping information provided the assurances for the marine insurance industry to flourish. By 1774 underwriters and brokers had secured premises on the upper floor of the Royal Exchange.

Meanwhile alongside London's trade and insurance functions, the city's modern commercial banking system emerged in the sixteenth century after King Henry VIII repealed the usury laws to allow money to be lent with interest. Italian merchants had a major impact on its early creation, being responsible for much of the industry's vocabulary: cash, debtor, creditor, and ledger. When Charles I seized all the gold being held in the Royal Mint, irreparably damaging the mint's reputation as a safe haven for assets, independent goldsmith bankers who held their own reserves in gold or silver soared in number. These goldsmiths founded many of London's most famous private banking institutions, and the network's credibility was maintained through dispersed reserves and monitors in London and other global cities. This system, which was complementary to Amsterdam's more centralized model, drove London's own model of financial innovation.

In 1694 the Bank of England was founded to manage the finances and the debt of the crown, and went on to dominate the national banking market throughout the eighteenth century. By the 1750s London had become a highly experimental financial

Continued

center in fairly symbiotic relationship with Amsterdam. But the corporate structure of the Bank of England gave London an advantage because its capital stock was concentrated rather than divided up among port cities as in Holland. This allowed the Bank of England and the New East India Company to increase their capital stock when necessary to meet the needs of stakeholders. Gradually, London's population continued to grow toward 1 million, whereas Amsterdam's stalled.

FIGURE 3-2.

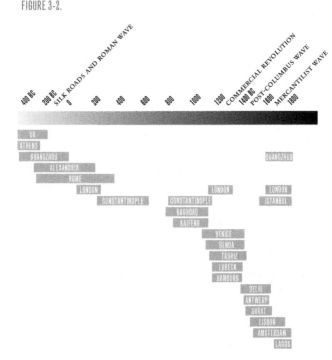

certain cities became externally oriented and the propensity of certain cities to reenter systems of trade on repeated occasions. Cities across these waves of globalization appear to share several commonalities in terms of drivers to become externally oriented and engage in long-distance exchange.

**Trade and connectivity.** Trade in particular kinds of goods and services empowered many cities in the premodern period to take active roles along trade routes and become specialized. Trade is the factor that was most correlated with the ability to globalize and with the type of city that was successful in globalizing. Basic products, natural resources, and natural capital were often the forces driving international commerce in cities. As early as the ninth century AD, tea was a traded commodity, spurring growth in Indian and Chinese cities, while the role of sugar in fuelling globalization across Europe and Asia is well documented.[16] The production of cotton drove the activities of cities as diverse as Bombay, Manchester, and Savannah. Silk, dyestuffs, iron, tobacco, and timber were also very important to the global cities of the seventeenth and eighteenth centuries.

**Entrepreneurial populations.** Demographic expansion and the mobility of populations were important drivers of globalizing cities in early waves. The expansion of Scythians into western and Central Asia was a major catalyst to long-distance trade, and later the ability of peasants to migrate into cities in preindustrial Europe boosted economic change and was linked to a broader expansion of trade.[17]

**Innovation and influence.** The ability to spread ideas was often critical to early global cities' soft and hard power. Cities often became more internationally engaged in tandem with the acceptance and application of new concepts and philosophies. Shared theological presumptions were undoubtedly an important undercurrent of many waves of globalization in the medieval and early modern periods.

**Discovery.** The encounter with new lands and the discovery of new viable travel routes have been catalysts for rapid change in global economic dynamics. The discovery of the Cape of Good Hope route to India in 1498 contributed to the rise of Portuguese, Dutch, and English cities and the relative decline of Mediterranean cities, as Europe's and Asia's markets became more closely integrated. Territorial expansion and colonization were a fundamental part of the creation of the global urban system, allowing new products to be traded and helping to forge new trade links along and across language barriers.

**Geopolitical opportunity.** Long periods of peace, decreased geopolitical conflict, or a change in the balance of military power have been catalysts propelling new groups of cities into the global arena. This is true even as far back as the Roman Empire. Later, in the eighth through to the eleventh centuries, the effects of Islamic conquest on the global economy and its systems of taxation and tribute are evident.[18] What is apparent is that in periods of instability, certain groups of cities that are viewed as having security advantages have often attracted merchants, entrepreneurs, and migrants in large numbers. In Europe, such cities often acquired reputations as sanctuaries for successive generations of people fleeing persecution. On the other side of the coin, geopolitical shifts and setbacks seriously derailed global cities' aspirations. Military defeats, a loss of allies, or long-term inertia in the wider region have all proved terminal for some of the leading global cities in history, from Baghdad to Venice and Antwerp.

In the premodern era up until the late eighteenth century, each wave of globalizing cities was different. Particular cities were in the vanguard, distinctive ideas were at the fore, and specific roles were played by business, armies, and government. This rich history reveals that the five elements observed increasingly emerge as the common features of the early global cities, though it was several centuries later before they were referred to as such.

# FOUR THE HISTORY OF GLOBAL CITIES II: MODERN CITIES

FOR MANY OBSERVERS OF urban history, the modern era of globalization began with industrialization, whose effects occurred at a pace and on a scale not previously seen. Although the globalization of traded goods long preceded the industrial era, industrialization really reshaped whole societies, not just the tastes of upper-income groups. By this point in history, in the late eighteenth century, national governments had become much more effective at managing global trade and reducing the dangers involved in carrying it out, while transport was becoming ever more reliable. These were the preconditions for successive waves of cities to become substantially more global in their traded specializations, diversify their populations, and increase their capacity for commercial innovation.

THE FIRST INDUSTRIAL WAVE: 1760–1850    A turning point in globalization occurred in the late eighteenth century owing
to a confluence of geopolitics and technological innovation. The victory of Britain in the Seven Years' War enhanced British power in India, and a more comprehensive
system of colonial government was installed. This situation favored British industrial development, and in 1771
the first water-powered cotton spinning model was in-
vented. At the same time, colonial disputes in North and
Central America intensified.

As a result, a new wave of cities globalized as part of the
British Empire. Undoubtedly the slave trade, managed from
London, was critical in financing British imperialism and
industrialization, and cities such as Bridgetown, Barbados,
and Kingston, Jamaica, became subject to the empire's
needs. As the empire extended its reach east, Cape Town,
Calcutta, and Hong Kong all became globally engaged
cities, with Calcutta subject to a system of mercantilism,
while Hong Kong became an instrument for promoting free
trade. In East Africa, Mombasa grew into an important
trade entrepôt with strong maritime business links to India
and the Arabian Peninsula, as well as the long-distance
caravan trade across East Africa.[1] Another city that became
open to global flows was Canton (box 4-1).

The British Empire likely had a greater impact on
global cities than any of its rivals, and many of the cities
enrolled in the imperial project remain highly influential
actors on the global stage today. London, New York,
Hong Kong, Singapore, Sydney, Mumbai, Shanghai,
Toronto, Cape Town, and Boston each developed their
global roles and reach within the British Empire.

BOX 4-1. GUANGZHOU: COMPELLED GLOBAL CITY

For nearly a thousand years, Guangzhou has been China's maritime gateway to the Middle East, India, and Southeast Asia. Under the Ming dynasty, its gateway role was deliberately restrained. By the late 1700s Guangzhou, or Canton, as it was then known, was the country's only platform for maritime trade with European merchants, and was kept under strict control.

Under a regime known as the "Guangzhou system," which ran for eighty years from 1760, Guangzhou was partially opened to foreign merchants, but under harsh restrictions. An imperial commissioner oversaw foreign exchanges and ensured that a Chinese merchant guild would retain the monopoly. The system allowed foreign traders to live only in specific areas just outside the city. Foreigners were forbidden to deal with the local population, and the prices on all imports and exports were strictly controlled. This placed overseas traders at a disadvantage, as the value of imports was deflated while exports were artificially made more costly.

Among the most valued goods was tea, a commodity whose popularity in Europe soared in the late eighteenth century. The quantity of tea (and other valued wares) bought in Guangzhou was such that Europeans were running out of silver to pay for it, silver being the main commodity the Chinese were willing to accept as payment. This precipitated a dark period in Guangzhou's history. In possession of superior commercial and military strength, Westerners were using the port to funnel opium illegally into China, which allowed them to pay for the silver they needed. As addiction rates soared and China sought to clamp down on the situation, the trade was cut off. European powers responded militarily and forced Guangzhou and other "treaty harbours" open in the so called Opium Wars from 1842 onward. Guangzhou went from being China's controlled global gateway to a foreign-controlled enclave— an example of a global city opened to the world by force.

Infrastructure connectivity was often the catalyst. One of the clearest examples of this was in New York. In 1825 a growth coalition between New York's city leaders and businesses began the construction of the Erie Canal, connecting the city to the Great Lakes and the U.S. Midwest. The availability of this water route resulted in a phenomenal surge in local manufacturing and trade and new financial and insurance industries supplying the growth of a young America. New York moved ahead of Philadelphia in financial power as a result of its enhanced connectivity.[2]

In Britain itself, cities such as Liverpool, Bristol, and Birmingham prospered from having access to imperial markets and from the global reach they afforded.[3] Manchester emerged as the world's first global industrial city. London, the city at the center of it all, surpassed Beijing's all-time population record, reaching 2 million by 1840. Across Europe, a wave of cities benefited from unprecedented urban growth and industrial expansion. The European cities that globalized in this wave had in common a specific set of assets: historical trading knowledge, locations on major rivers or seas, and the ready availability of natural resources such as coal, iron, and water. Drawing on this asset base, places such as Bilbao, Bremen, Leipzig, Sheffield, and Turin were able to build exceptional manufacturing economies, specializing in engineering, machine tools, ships, and other industrial areas. They attracted a huge manufacturing labor force and became pioneering cities in terms of their public services, education, and civic institutions.

Other cities in this wave of globalization flourished as centers of artistic creativity and diversity. Vienna drew intellectuals and enthusiastic artists, and fostered classical geniuses such as Mozart, Haydn, and Shubert. Music was

FIGURE 4-1. **GRABEN LUXURY SHOPPING STREET IN VIENNA, 1895**

Source: Josef Löwy (Wiki Commons).

a major cultural asset for the city and gave it regional influence. The Vienna Conference of 1814–15 redrew the map of Europe and underscored the city's diplomatic clout. As the capital of the Austro-Hungarian Empire, Vienna became a major investor in the region and a haven for immigrants of numerous backgrounds. By 1900, 60 percent of its population was thought to be foreign-born.[4]

**THE MASS INDUSTRY WAVE: 1850–1914**   Economic globalization expanded massively in the decades leading up to World War I. One of the main groups of cities to globalize in this wave was in the United States. American cities became substantially differentiated and specialized at this time, with their own mix of industrial enterprises and the "second wave" of immigration giving them very different

## BOX 4-2. LOS ANGELES: GLOBAL CITY OF ENTERTAINMENT

Los Angeles was one of the cities to benefit most from the late nineteenth-century expansion of globalization. The arrival of rail in Kansas City in 1876 had opened it up to the interior U.S. economy and it began to overtake San Francisco as the topography of

### HOLLYWOOD STUDIOS IN 1922

social and cultural characters. New York specialized in advanced services and consumer products, Chicago became a center for heavy industrial plants, while Los Angeles moved into oil and the creative industries (box 4-2). Diverse and entrepreneurial populations played an indispensable role: New York was the main U.S. gateway for immigrant labor. Tens of millions of immigrants, mainly Europeans, came to the city, and many settled there in the region made rail and later road connections a lot easier. By the 1940s it had emerged as America's second global city.

An agricultural depression in the 1890s was the trigger for diversification. An aqueduct and a deep sea port were built thanks to active business lobbying for federal grants. Los Angeles became the closest U.S. port city to the new Panama Canal and by the late 1920s it was handling over 26 million tons of cargo. Its aviation and automobile clusters took on a regional dimension, while the discovery of oil made it a significant global producer. It was also a hub for immigration from China, Japan, and Mexico, and the city reached 1 million by 1920.

Oil, aircraft production, and in particular the film industry were the levers by which Los Angeles built and sustained its global presence. The city's climate and scenery became an attraction for the movie industry, and in 1911 the first Hollywood studio opened. By the 1930s the motion picture industry had exploded into a global cultural phenomenon and was the city's largest employer, with 30-40,000 workers. Los Angeles thus became one of the cultural capitals of the twentieth century—where the American Dream was marketed to the world.

search of a better life, making New York a cosmopolitan city on a scale never previously seen. Infrastructure was a critical enabler for this wave of American city globalization. The installation of canals, railroads, water systems, highways, and sewerage systems helped to provide the conditions for a half century of extraordinary growth.[5]

Cities were also places of discovery and invention in this wave of globalization. The numerous advances in technology in the 1860s and 1870s included Alexander Parkes's invention of the first plastic, in Birmingham; Louis Pasteur's development of the pasteurization process, in Paris; Alexander Graham Bell's crafting of the telephone in a laboratory in Boston; and Charles Parsons's building of the steam turbine in Newcastle, England. These technologies unleashed huge changes in the industrial and urban fabrics of many cities in North America and Europe and intensified the exchange of ideas and innovations.

## THE POSTWAR WAVE AND THE RESURGENCE IN GLOBAL TRADE: 1945–1973

A major wave of cities taking on global roles unfolded in the aftermath of World War II. Changing geopolitics and American investment support provided opportunities for many commercially minded cities to become highly specialized. Often benefiting from sound city leadership, cities in this wave of globalization were successful in restoration and in planning ahead to avoid the worst in congestion.

Munich, Toronto, and Tokyo are all prominent examples of cities in this wave (box 4-3). These cities were able to achieve intensive clustering and organizational modernization in a supportive political environment among higher tiers of government. For this wave it was key for corporate proficiency to partner with a strong knowledge platform in order to develop successful products for export. Cities in this wave of globalization were prominent well into the mid-1970s, by which time they had acquired many of the core assets that make them competitive today. Although these cities have experienced slowdowns and setbacks in the last twenty-five years, they have successfully preserved

BOX 4-3. TOKYO: FROM MEGACITY TO GLOBAL CITY

From very unpromising geopolitical circumstances, Tokyo really became a global city after 1945. Its economic growth strategy was based on dramatic industrial expansion that owed to close relationships between the state and private business, which spawned massive industrial conglomerates. With the Bank of Japan increasing its lending limits, Tokyo's firms were able to leverage advanced production techniques to generate an enormous volume of exports and establish Japan's capital as a major industrial and commercial center. Tokyo's pathway to globalization was more dependent on nationally designed reforms than on metro-level intentionality. It was an early example of a pattern that would be repeated later by Asian nations that deliberately set out to globalize their largest cities.

Tokyo's industry evolved from mass production to high-tech flexible specialization in the 1970s, and profitable links between large firms and small and medium-sized entities were forged. State controls on imports and on foreign investment meant that the city's economy was dominated by Japanese companies financed by Japanese banks. The city was less a global meeting place or cultural center than a highly successful platform for national export industries. Of the 500 largest Japanese industrial firms in 1975, only 33 were multinationals. The city first became strategic about its global roles in the 1980s with the liberalization reforms of the Nakasone premiership, when many of Tokyo's leading corporations and financial institutions set up operations overseas. More recently Tokyo and Japan's governments have proactively restated their ambitions to remain among the leading group of global cities. Their Special Zones initiatives to

Continued

expand the Central Business District to host global companies and entrepreneurs contrast with efforts in the past to decentralize and deconcentrate the capital. Now the aim is to reduce the rigidities in national policies that are inhibiting the city's ability to react to a fast changing system of cities in Asia.

Innovation within a well-organized institutional culture has been at the heart of Tokyo's global export success. The city has drawn on a large pool of Japanese talent for its labor market, and the standard of education and training in Japanese educational institutions has been consistently high, boosted by very good links between academia and business. The transfer of R&D into commercially viable products is said to reflect a high degree of market understanding and respect for the commercial process ingrained in the culture of learning in Tokyo.

a culture of knowledge and innovation to support specializations with global reach.

Perhaps the most remarkable example during this wave was Singapore, the only global city also to be a fully autonomous city-state. Prior to independence in 1965, Singapore's economic prospects were uncertain. Its traditional entrepôt trade industries had declined, manufacturing was stagnant, and housing and roads were in urgent need of modernization. But its first prime minister, Lee Kuan Yew, was not deterred by geographic limitations and immediately pursued a labor-intensive industrialization policy that was open to overseas capital. Emphasis was placed on tax incentives for industrial investors, improved labor discipline, technical education, and foreign expertise in order to specialize in industrial technologies. Singapore immediately tried to build trade and connectivity roles by leveraging its position as a multilingual city, with links to East and West and a strong Western legal model. Since achieving global status, Singapore has continued to adapt to the global marketplace through state-led policies and programs that encourage light manufacturing and high-technology research investment. Its Economic Development Board and Housing Development Board in particular have been able to leverage the scale of large public institutions to create effective systems at a citywide scale. Singapore's experience shows how recently globalizing cities can overcome inherited disadvantages and maximize advantages in the global economy. Today Singapore has come to exemplify many of the quintessential characteristics of a global city with its broad-based prosperity, stability, openness, deep networks, and leading-edge innovation. It serves as an inspiration and a model for other aspiring globalizing cities.

The postwar wave of globalization was also striking for the process of decolonization, which saw many cities lose their imperial roles. In the past, many global cities fell along with the empires that spawned them. Indeed, for London this period coincided with a challenging postwar process of deindustrialization, port decline, and outdated regulation in its stock exchange, banking, and insurance sectors. Although London attracted immigrants from the Commonwealth diaspora, the city continued to lose population until the mid-1980s, when it resumed the journey toward becoming a quintessential global city. In their own ways, Paris, Madrid, and Lisbon also retain regional spheres of influence.

## THE ICT-POWERED WAVE OF
## LIBERALIZATION: 1985–2007
The decade after the 1973 oil
crisis and the subsequent global slowdown was a period
of great flux in the global economy. Older models became
discredited and new ideas and solutions came to the fore.
By the mid-1980s a new wave of globalization was under
way, led initially by a small group of cities but with an
increasing number of smaller cities also becoming globally engaged and globally oriented for the first time.

For a small, elite group of financial centers, the mid-
1980s started a wave of resurgence when these cities
began to reattract population, business, and capital. London and New York began to reverse their population
decline, and in London the 1986 "Big Bang" in financial
services marked the start of a new generation of international banks and surrounding business services firms
setting up shop. This cadre of cities sought to adjust their
regulatory framework with the help of their national governments to offer attractive access to international markets and to capture new sources of foreign direct investment. Their globalization of financial services triggered
large-scale redevelopment to build capacity, and also encouraged diversified growth in media and R&D.[6]

For Asian members of this group, such as Tokyo and
Singapore, this wave was characterized by a more selective
and tactical globalization that promoted internationalization of financial and business sectors through liberalization reforms while also protecting against overexposure to
Western cultural influences.

In this wave of globalization cities also reestablished
themselves as information and media capitals in their

respective regions. This period was notable for significant governance changes in some cities, such as the abolition and then the re-creation of a metropolitan government system in London; the new "one country, two systems" policy in Hong Kong, which sought to guarantee that it would maintain a capitalist system for fifty years after the 1997 British handover to China; and the increasing withdrawal of federal government from its role in New York City.

At the same time, the new wave of globalization was showcasing a set of cities that until then had not been globally oriented. The global geopolitical context had changed considerably as a result of the fall of communism in Europe, the unification of Germany, the opening up of China beginning in 1980, and the Oslo Peace Accords, part of the Arab-Israeli Peace Process, in 1993. The agreements of new trade arrangements, such as the European Economic Area and the North American Free Trade Association, and the establishment of the World Trade Organization in 1995 ushered in an era of multilateralism that allowed many countries and cities to globalize. All these factors created a climate of opportunity for the growth of leading cities in the BRICS (Brazil, Russia, India, China, and South Africa) and the smaller MINTs (Mexico, Indonesia, Nigeria, Turkey) economies, as well as in eastern Europe, the Middle East, and Australasia. Among the most notable cities coming to global prominence in this wave were Bangalore, Barcelona, Cape Town, Sydney, and Tel Aviv.

**Tradable specializations.** New tradable specializations associated with the information and communications technology (ICT) revolution precipitated the unexpected globalization of many cities. Bangalore is one of the most striking examples. Its electronics specialization took off in 1985 after the arrival of Texas Instruments. This prompted other multinational firms to relocate and boosted the local software design environment, laying the platform for successive climbs up the value chain. Bangalore's shift from outsourcing to offshore services was spurred by firms upgrading production processes and procuring higher skill functions. Indian government support to upgrade the data communications infrastructure and tax regime to fuel growth and advance skills development was key, as was the World Bank's sponsorship of new development agencies to manage new infrastructure development. Bangalore is an example of a city in this wave for which specialization has yielded more intentional global awareness and a common agenda for growth among local firms and entrepreneurs.

The reorganization of a city's trade system was an important precondition for many cities globalizing in this wave. Seattle is an example of a metropolitan area that overcame political fragmentation to ensure its aerospace and technology sectors could stay competitive. The Trade Development Alliance of Greater Seattle (TDA) was founded in 1991 to coordinate the city's international activities and to promote the region in international markets. Seattle became one of the most advanced cities in North America at supporting companies, managing delegations from overseas, and linking small businesses with foreign opportunities. A culture of international learning and visits was embedded that has made Seattle's leaders highly responsive to how the city is positioned in the global marketplace.

**Innovation and influence.** The leverage of innovation and influence was an important ingredient for globalizing cities that were one step removed from core markets. These cities tended to have knowledge assets but a mainly public sector–led research or manufacturing base. In the 1980s they sought to reposition their economy internationally and build new sources of economic demand. Often a single event played a catalytic role: the arrival of Texas Instruments in Bangalore in 1985 sparked the growth of the software sector, Barcelona's successful bid to host the Olympic Games provided the impetus for physical rejuvenation, and the creation of the Sydney Stock Exchange in 1987 saw Sydney emerge as a leading regional financial center. Others, such as San Francisco, became centers of innovation aided by a deep and nonhierarchical culture of knowledge exchange (box 4-4).

One of the most striking examples of innovation driving a city's globalization in this wave comes from Tel Aviv. This young city's spirit of commerce and entrepreneurial capitalism translated into an open and horizontal concentration of skills in finance, optics, communications, information systems, medicine, and software. This strong technological base was reinforced by the Israeli military's investment in the city's advanced defense industries, which produced a regular flow of highly proficient talent. With its tech cluster benefiting from a supportive early-stage investor arrangement and a positive attitude to risk, Tel Aviv has become noted for its numerous tech inventions. The city's leadership has since sought to reinforce this global potential by emphasizing Tel Aviv's pluralism, tolerance, and investment readiness.

BOX 4-4. SAN FRANCISCO: CITY OF DISCOVERY AND INNOVATION

San Francisco's status as a global city stems from the fact it has created the world's most powerful innovation system of advanced services, tech firms, and startups. Historically associated with opportunity after the 1848–55 gold rush, in World War II San Francisco was the world's largest shipyard. The region relied on its large port and comprehensive rail connectivity to retain its position as a gateway to Asia. But by the 1970s the microelectronics revolution in Silicon Valley had fundamentally changed the global role of San Francisco.

Silicon Valley relied largely on San Francisco's network of financial institutions to fund new startups. A steady flow of talented workers anchored by advanced research institutions, accessible venture capital, a welcoming culture, and high quality of life proved the key to a virtuous cycle of success. Spatial clustering was highly effective, including in biotech, with firms such as Genentech established next to the University of San Francisco. The city's businesses viewed globalization and environmental regulation as an opportunity rather than a threat. As the need for flexible, diverse networks was recognized, interactions between firms were very regular, and the Bay Area Council played a central networking role. The long-term outcome was that between 1970 and 2010, San Francisco's IT workforce grew from 2.7 percent to 10.2 percent of the city's employees, and the city's per capita income is now 30 percent higher than that of neighboring Los Angeles.[a]

During the 1990s and 2000s, San Francisco merged with San Jose's Silicon Valley to form the world's most productive area for technology research and innovation. It gained a global reputation as a technologically driven, entrepreneurial, cosmopolitan, diverse city that supplied a unique pool of smart, open-minded workers. The city boasts world-class research universities and iconic cultural and tourist attractions. It exports a substantial share of petroleum, coal, and chemicals, as well as business services, tourism, and electronics.

SAN FRANCISCO IN 1982

San Francisco has a diversified platform for competitiveness in the twenty-first century. Its high-tech economy boasts one of America's leading biotechnology and biomedical clusters, anchored by the University of California–San Francisco. UCSF and UC–Berkeley lead a contingent of colleges and universities that attract thousands of international students and produce cutting-edge research and development. San Francisco has also invested in its natural beauty, iconic design and architecture, and its arts and cultural institutions in order to attract skilled workers and tourists. City and business leaders have worked hard to establish a very positive economic relationship with China, spanning manufacturing, universities, and foreign direct investment.

This wave of globalization was distinctive for a more intentional approach by city governments and the rise of strategic planning for globalizing cities. For cities like Barcelona and Tel Aviv, city governments designed strategic approaches to infrastructure, quality of life, and architecture in order to build a profile that would attract global talent. Many also converted their commercial land into use by more innovation-led activity. In nearly all cases, these cities witnessed an unprecedented wave of population diversification, fueled by immigration and mobile talent. By the climax of this wave in 2007–08, these cities had a totally different global proposition—and new problems that had appeared alongside growth.

This twenty- to twenty-five-year wave of globalization was also a time of great change and reform for larger cities in middle-income countries. In cities such as Shanghai, Istanbul, and Seoul, newly empowered city leadership sought to drive change in the physical urban fabric and attract foreign investment much more actively to increase and maintain economic development. A number of cities radically improved their political and legal framework, with the support of national governments. The quality and accountability of these cities' leaderships were in many cases also transformed during this time, and the net result was a group of cities that were much more open to global influence, developing new spaces for consumption, and increasing opportunities for large-scale real estate and service industry investment. Existing specializations were amplified, notably in banking and insurance, logistics, the automotive sector, and science. Powerful and charismatic mayors driving rapid change were a hallmark of this wave.

**THE CURRENT WAVE: 2008–PRESENT**  The most recent cycle of globalization has seen the start of a new wave of distinctive, specialized, and globally aspirational cities. Many of them are higher-income cities within their respective regions and seek to leverage their efficient infrastructure, improved quality of life, and better security and environmental performance compared to the larger megacities. Cities in this wave are less likely to have major political or institutional functions. Rather, they are competing in more dynamic and fast-moving global industries where opportunities have arisen for greater market share. Among this group are Brisbane, San Diego, Shenzhen, Santiago de Chile, and Stockholm.

There is a clear set of drivers for cities in this latest wave of globalization. The first is that many industries have become a lot more footloose than was ever anticipated. Previously it was assumed that research institutions, universities, hospitals and health clusters, screen industries, and others were fixed permanently in one place, but now increasing mobility and hybridity characterize these sectors. At the same time, technology is changing business models and adding flexibility to the nature of supply chains and value chains.

In the aftermath of the global financial crisis and its impact on public sector finances, the ability of cities to find new sources and tools for investment has been a key enabler for globalizing cities since 2008. Brisbane is an example of a city that has been able to globalize with the help of a large and financially astute city government, which has used the surplus from its recent commodities boom to erect a more international model of economic development.

The Brisbane City Council has pursued a wide range of joint ventures, sponsored business conventions and sporting events, and convinced its state government to prioritize Brisbane for road and rail infrastructure funding. It has also experimented with public-private partnerships and toll roads, with some success. Much of the city's investment attractiveness owes to its reputation in Asia, where its Ambassadors program has boosted expatriate investment connections and reached out much more successfully to Chinese, Japanese, and Malaysian commodities firms.

The ability to attract a new generation of immigrants and entrepreneurs has been central to many cities' success in this wave. The ability to convey opportunity and appeal to the world, whether to talent, investors, or visitors, has also been very important. London is an example of a city that has been successful in this area since 2008. Through a unified organization, London & Partners, it has delivered a consistent message to the world that it is open for business and investment and has made substantial strides in becoming a city that welcomes new technology and science industries. In medicine, media, and digital industries the ingredients of leading sector innovations, combined with an open city with deep labor markets and cosmopolitan livability, have created a winning formula. The city's advocacy organizations have helped maintain its appeal by successfully lobbying for a competitive business and tax climate.

SUMMARY   A comparison of the waves of globalization in the last two centuries with the earlier waves featured in chapter 2 shows clearly that the duration of each wave is becoming shorter. Where waves once lasted a century or more, they now appear to run their course in as little as fifteen to twenty years, and in the future this duration may be even shorter. As the global economy becomes ever more integrated, globalizing city waves increasingly come to resemble global economic cycles, and the windows of opportunity for cities to participate close quickly.

Previous globalizing city waves highlight that the phenomenon of cities entering into competition with each other stretches back much further than the last half century. We see repeated examples of city leaders deliberately trying to create more attractive conditions for commerce and using their soft power to shape and determine the rules of the game.

Although there are vast differences between the networks of cities along the ancient Silk Roads and the twenty-first-century system of global value chains and competitive advantage, there are also many striking parallels. Several salient ones are highlighted below.

## Specialization in Globally Traded Sectors

In each wave, new cities succeed in gaining access to and specializing in globally traded sectors. Privileged access to trade has been a key feature in waves of globalization in the modern period. Usually this access has been achieved through imperial power, strategic location, or infrastructure development. London's role as a gateway to empire was indispensable to the development of its unique trade ties and cultural influence. Its imperial functions made it a place where the wealthy and the ambitious from around the world congregated to learn and trade, and where numerous innovations in finance were developed and refined. In a different way, New York's initial globalization was triggered by opportunities to participate in the Atlantic trade and was boosted by the decision to build the Erie Canal, which positioned New York as a hub connecting the agricultural and industrial output of the U.S. Midwest to the rest of the world.

Certain traded industries played an outsized role in each wave of globalization. Extractive industries, textiles, and automotive manufacturing were among the important sectors in the post-1945 wave. Finance and media were the sectors behind globalization in the 1980s and 1990s. In the current wave, since 2008–09, the internationalization of medicine, higher education, and clean technology, among many other sectors, has played a prominent role. Each city has different institutional and business capabilities to take advantage of globalization in different industries. Others that used to rely principally on trade also tend to diversify into other forms of economic models and gain other kinds of influence.

The origins of traded specializations vary, and in many cases in the modern period national governments played a decisive catalytic role. State-led industrial expansion has been essential to the globalization of most Asian global cities. National government support and nationally designed reforms to deliberately globalize played a larger role than in the previous business ecosystems. The ability to compete on both volume and quality was a key part of the export strategy for cities such as Seoul, Singapore, and Tokyo in the 1945–73 wave and played a similar role for globalizing Chinese cities in the 1985–2008 wave. The rapid evolution from mass production to higher-value R&D and innovation functions has enabled these cities to diversify their global relationships over time.

Not all cities have made this transition successfully, and their success in doing so appears to be linked to the commercial awareness and professionalism of the leading institutions. Higher-order functions have also allowed these cities to become centers for decisionmaking and high-quality cultural and educational institutions.

*Entrepreneurial, Diverse Populations*

Entrepreneurial and diverse populations with strong natural or established links to other cities and regions have been a constant source of trade advantage. Global cities that show themselves open to people, ideas, and knowledge have tended to attract scholars, intellectuals, and innovators, who then fuel the next generation of productive growth.

Large-scale migration has been critical to diversifying a city's global ties in the last two centuries. The large-scale immigration of populations into American cities between 1880 and 1950 was an important source of new trade links and commercial and intellectual ideas.

The arrival of immigrant populations in cities has been a common denominator for global cities such as London, New York, Istanbul, and Hong Kong. For immigration did more than solve labor shortages and drive entrepreneurship and trade ties. That these cities have successively hosted refugees, revolutionaries, and exiles has also given them a status in their region as safe havens for people and capital, which is a major advantage, especially during periods of financial and political uncertainty. Other globalizing cities have also experienced their own story of demographic change. In the last forty years, large-scale rural-urban migration in cities across Latin America and China has enabled industries to compete on cost and to enter global value chains.

### Discovery of New Markets, Routes, Products, and Services

The discovery of new markets, routes, products, and services has been a key driver of new trade routes and of new cities engaging in long-distance exchange, while often also changing the balance of power between groups of cities. The discovery of gold in California was critical to San Francisco's emergence as a Pacific center for trade, finance, and shipyard production. The discovery of oil and gas and the development of techniques of extraction literally fueled the ways in which industrializing cities traded and communicated and brought commodities-rich cities into the global orbit. Oil-rich cities such as Cairo, Jakarta, and Kuala Lumpur became global investment locations in the wave after 1945, while in the post-2008 wave such cities as Abu Dhabi, Brisbane, Perth, and Calgary have leveraged their oil and gas wealth to take on new global functions. Today, globalization is also characterized by growing regulatory powers and responsibilities around the use of natural resources, and a new wave of cities plays a prominent role in the sustainable and responsible use of resources.

Discovery takes on a rather different meaning and dimension in the modern technological era. Rather than discovering new territories or minerals, cities globalize from the development of new services or techniques.

High-end producer services such as accountancy, advertising, consultancy, and legal services have grown at a phenomenal rate in the cycles since 1980 because of their role in underpinning firms' export and expansion plans. Services for the real estate industry have also been prominent since the mid-1990s. Retail, hospitality, entertainment, and technology services are an important phenomenon in the current wave and in many respects constitute a form of discovery of their own.

*Innovation and Influence*
New technologies, new ideas, and the ability to shape opinion and action have been important parts of modern waves. Schools of economic thought, from mercantilism to classical political economy, from Marx to the Chicago school, also enrolled cities in new practices and regulations over the past 400 years. Transformative ideas such as natural selection, popular democracy, and even the notion of a free press have stimulated the vibrancy and growth of cities at key junctures throughout history. Step changes in technology in particular have been essential to the way cities perceive themselves and their international roles in the last two centuries. Cities in the first industrial wave developed and shared a new set of innovations in the production process. Transport innovations were at the forefront. The railway in particular allowed people, goods, capital, and ideas to be much more rapidly transported, and overhauled the spatial structure of nearly all cities by the early twentieth century. Communications technologies have enabled the kind of agglomeration processes to occur that allow cities to expand their productivity. More recently, the containerization of shipping is one

innovation that has transformed the fortunes of port cities and prompted new industrial and postindustrial strategies for cities, as has the rise in ICT and mobile technology. New developments in media, computing, and finance have been important to certain cities becoming influential in twentieth- and twenty-first- century waves.

In the modern period, the ways in which cities build a successful environment for innovation and internationalize their economies through them are much debated. For San Francisco, a mature horizontal network of companies supported by a pool of financial institutions helped new start-ups to thrive in the first instance. What is clear is that high-quality research institutions, good air and freight connections, and attractive urban design and amenities are important for centers of innovation to flourish in the modern global economy.

## Geopolitical Opportunities

Geopolitical opportunities have continued to play a part in enabling cities to become or remain global in their outlook and capability. The fall of communism, the signing of peace agreements, political transitions, or changes in the balance of power are also important drivers that favor a different group of cities. The impact of war shaped the global roles of certain cities in the twentieth century. New York City's role as a source of financial capital expanded dramatically after the destruction of World Wars I and II in Europe, while Tokyo's reindustrialization after 1945 was given added impetus and urgency by the huge wartime damage it suffered. After 1945, soaring peacetime demand in the U.S. sphere of influence saw cities such as

Munich and Toronto become specialized exporters. Soon after, the breakup of the British Commonwealth was a stimulus for British cities and cities in Africa and South Asia to form new trade networks. Later, the geopolitical events of 1989–91, when the Soviet Union dissolved and Germany unified, also ushered in new regional economic agreements and so triggered the globalization of cities as varied as Vienna, Warsaw, Tel Aviv, and Vancouver.

The recent period has seen new cities benefit from geopolitical changes, including Beijing, Hong Kong, Miami, and Santiago de Chile. Regime changes at the national level or an end to civil conflict have been preconditions for cities such as Barcelona, Bogota, Cape Town, and Colombo to build a strategic international approach. When cities emerge from relative detachment or isolation, tourism often becomes an important strategy to attract new audiences to a city, giving the city the confidence to trade and compete.

By contrast, in many cities in the twentieth and twenty-first centuries politics and international engagement have been constrained by totalitarianism, conflict, instability, or corruption, although others, such as cities with a large commodities base (for example, Dubai, Brisbane, or Santiago de Chile), have become more global because of the price booms associated with conflict.

The lesson to be drawn from this short history of waves of global cities, past and present, is that global cities come in many guises. Some are founded on political and imperial power, but most have been something else: dynamic centers of commerce, culturally eclectic knowledge hubs, highly specialized single-sector exporters, or capitals of creativity. There is much for cities in the present to learn from how cities in previous waves built and sustained their competitive attributes, and how to avoid becoming locked into unsustainable or unproductive cycles of development.

Not all of today's leading cities were destined from the start to play key roles in the global economy. Many started out from an unpromising or uncompetitive situation because of either internal weaknesses or external disadvantages. Sometimes cities have endured long periods of global isolation and begin to internationalize only when geopolitical changes occur and foreign investment arrives. This was certainly the case in the twentieth century, and in the twenty-first century it is visible in many other cities outside the established West.

Equally, the ebb and flow of cities' fortunes means that some cities that we take for granted today as global will likely be much less globally oriented in future. History shows this is a risk if cities lose competitiveness in traded sectors, fail to embrace innovation or to project influence, are closed to immigration and entrepreneurship, or are unable to adapt to a changing geopolitical or geoeconomic center of gravity.

The ingredients of today's most successful cities are sometimes hard for other cities to emulate directly, and so alternative strategies and pathways to global engagement have arisen. Over time, these alternative pathways result in different kinds of global cities, as explained in chapter 6.

# FIVE UNDERSTANDING GLOBAL CITIES

THINKING AND THEORIZING ABOUT the known world of urban settlements is as old as civilization itself. In each era, the frame of reference for understanding cities has broadly reflected the extent of the known world. For Rome and the capitals of the Chinese dynasties, this known world referred to all the civilized parts of their empires, outside which knowledge was only blurry and a perception of "barbarians" reigned. There was no strong sense of "global" as we understand it today, of continents connected by trade, shared values, and interests. Even "international" was a modern idea that arose with the consolidation of the nation-state. Yet an understanding of a city as a population aggregation with cross-cultural relevance, trade links, and connectivity goes back thousands of years.[1]

The first explicit references to "world cities" or "global cities" appeared around the time of World War I.

Many of these early statements or speculations originated in the United States and western Europe. The 1911 Annual Report of Chicago's City Planning Department refers to the advantages of being placed among "the front ranks of those world cities which are seriously bent upon the best and noblest work of which man is capable."[2] In his 1913 book, *Great Cities in America,* the city government expert Delos Franklin Wilcox referred to Chicago as among the "world cities of first rank," while Philadelphia was "*the* American city," distinct from "the world-cities that have grown up on American soil."[3] Meanwhile, in the same year on the other side of the Atlantic, Paris was described poetically as a "world city" that was a "cathedral of a new fast-paced world."[4]

But it is the town planner Patrick Geddes who is generally credited with formalizing the term *world cities* in his 1915 book, *Cities in Evolution.* Geddes was prescient in highlighting that electricity and the combustion engine were catalysts for city growth and aggregation over larger metropolitan areas. He cited as world cities not just the national and imperial capitals but also the emerging metro regions of "Tyne-Wear-Tees," the French Riviera, Düsseldorf, and Pittsburgh.[5]

In the 1920s and 1930s books and periodicals began more frequently to refer to Berlin, Vienna, London, and New York as world cities, especially in Europe. Sometimes drawing on the slightly different meanings of "*ville mondiale*" or "*Weltstadt,*" these references sought to capture the fact that certain cities were becoming cosmopolitan capitals, centers of culture as much as of commerce.[6] There are even allusions to the potential of Tangiers and Tunis to become world cities.[7] As a result, as early

**FIGURE 5-1. USAGE OF THE TERMS *GLOBAL CITY* AND *WORLD CITY* IN TWENTIETH-CENTURY BOOKS, AS PERCENTAGE SHARE OF BOOKS PUBLISHED IN EACH YEAR**

Source: Figure created with Google Ngram Viewer.

as 1930 the German Jewish writer Paul Cohen-Portheim was able to observe in a book about Paris that

> world city is a much misused term. A city may have several millions of inhabitants without being a world city; it is not numbers or area that decide, but importance. . . . London is a world city to-day because it is the centre of a realm to which a quarter of the earth's inhabitants belong.[8]

In the years that followed, the use of the term world city remained fairly sporadic and the term itself ill-defined. The term global city had not gained currency at all (figure 5-1). One of the first references invokes Detroit, described as "a global city in its concepts" because it was a producer of world-class air and highway transport technology.[9] It was not until the postwar peace, the movement toward decolonization, and the rapid shrinking of space and time in the telecommunications era of the 1960s that a new way of thinking about the global city began to take hold. At first this interest in cities merely reflected the appearance of large cities in which much of the world's business was being conducted. One of the key attributes embodied in such centres of business activity was cosmopolitan diversity. This appeared to point to a new role for the leading cities, as explained by Lewis Mumford in his 1961 classic, *The City in History*.

> The mission of the city in the global village is to hand onto the smallest urban unit the cultural resources that make for world unity and co-operation. . . . [The big city] has brought together, within relatively narrow compass, the diversity and variety of special cultures: at least in token quantities all races and cultures can be found here, along with their languages, their customs, their costumes, their typical cuisines: here the representatives of mankind first met face to face on neutral ground. . . . Unconsciously the great capitals have been preparing mankind for the wider associations and unifications which the modern conquest of time and space has made probable, if not inevitable.[10]

Much of the thinking on the world's melting pot cities was taking place as the Cold War unfolded, when national territories were absolutely primary and hierarchies between nations were the biggest shapers of the world system. The attributes of global cities were often understood more as an inevitable outcome of geopolitical shifts than as saying much about the cities themselves.[11] The national dimension was very much visible when Peter Hall published *The World Cities* in 1966, the first time that the phenomenon of urbanization and globalization was addressed head-on.[12] Hall argued that world cities were not just political and decisionmaking centers but also centers of trade, connectivity, talent, knowledge, information, and specialization. Hall's work set the stage for the modern study of cities undergoing globalization to blossom.

MODERN NOTIONS OF GLOBAL CITIES   The modern systematic thinking about global cities has unfolded in roughly three distinct but overlapping phases (table 5-1).

*The First Phase*
The *world city* as an analytical concept was developed in the 1970s and caught on in the 1980s as a new frame within which to grasp globalization. The idea emerged from the apparent paradox that in the age of IT and finance, economic activity was increasingly centralized in a handful of hub locations. A preeminent or "disproportionate" role for key cities has been a long-standing idea in sociology and geography, but the specific notion of cities steering the global economy can be traced to a small number of geographers and economists in the 1970s who were researching sites for the headquarters of multinational corporations.[13] For example, the Canadian economist Stephen Hymer in 1972 argued that "the world's major cities—New York, Paris, Bonn, London, Tokyo . . . along with

TABLE 5-1. **THREE WAVES OF GLOBAL CITY THEORY**

| | PROMINENT THINKERS | KEY IDEAS | PROMINENT CITIES |
|---|---|---|---|
| First wave | Peter Hall<br>David Heenan<br>John Friedmann<br>Goetz Wolff | Qualitative: multinational firms, international divisions of labor, knowledge command posts | Brussels<br>Frankfurt<br>London<br>New York<br>Randstad<br>Tokyo |
| Second wave | Saskia Sassen<br>Peter Taylor<br>Jonathan Beaverstock | Quantitative: financial services command points, specialized producer services, social polarization | London<br>New York<br>Tokyo<br>Followed by:<br>Los Angeles<br>Cities in global south |
| Third wave | Allen Scott<br>Michele Acuto<br>Christian Lefèvre<br>Jennifer Robinson | City regions, more global cities, transnational and global city policy networks, city-states, national governments | London<br>New York<br>Paris<br>Tokyo<br>Hong Kong<br>Singapore<br>Seoul<br>Shanghai<br>50–100 others |

Moscow and perhaps Peking, will be the major centers of high-level strategic planning." The rest would be "subordinate."[14] Unlike Hall's work, which still attributed power to states, this new school of thinking viewed global cities as at the top of a hierarchy whose corporate leaders effectively determined the fortunes of other cities. This shift in referential frame set the tone for the subsequent research agenda, which was primarily critical in perspective.

David A. Heenan, writing in the *Harvard Business Review*, is credited with using the term "global city" in 1977.[15] Global cities soon became popularized as an analytical concept when John Friedmann and Goetz Wolff set out a series of groundbreaking hypotheses in "World City Formation: An Agenda for Research and Action." For them, multinational firms had become footloose and were engaged in a bitter struggle for supremacy pitched around the big cities. They proposed "a new look at cities from the perspective of the world economic system-in-formation."[16]

At the time, the global city concept was mainly a qualitative and conceptual one. The idea of a system requirement for core cities to control and coordinate the world economy held a powerful appeal for the neo-Marxist inflection of urban studies and came to underpin the essential claims of all the subsequent literature.[17] The concept of a world city helped make sense of the Washington Consensus of free-market reform that was rapidly propelling the economies of developed nations toward finance, services, and reurbanization.[18] Emerging citadels of finance—London, New York, Tokyo—were thought of as command posts in the latest stage of capitalism. This phenomenon was widely viewed as unique, or at least unusual. As urban scholars Peter Taylor and Ben Derudder explain, "world empires were ultimately held together politically by armies, the modern world-system has been and continues to be held together economically through the worldwide link of cities."[19]

*The Second Phase*

Research on global cities took a step forward in the 1990s with Saskia Sassen's publication of *The Global City* in 1991.[20] Sassen theorized that only a handful of cities had the gravitational pull to operate as organizing centers for contemporary globalization. This elite group had developed unique densities of advanced services provision that offered financial, professional, and creative proficiency to corporate clients. As large firms became global, supporting services in such fields as commercial law, wealth management, corporate tax advice, and advertising sprang up around them in these urban centers. Correlatively, by the early 1990s the global city concept had also been accepted by business and policy communities. Among the first examples was a 1991 U.K. government report titled *London: World City Moving into the 21st Century.*[21] The report accepted the premise that London was competing with a small number of other leading cities and had to adjust its infrastructure and promotional activities accordingly.

In 2001, when Sassen updated her work, London, New York, and Tokyo were still the exemplary global cities, but now twenty or so other cities in the world economy were also providing similar services to global capital, if at a less concentrated level. By 2006, she observed:

about 40 major and not-so-major global cities . . . [which] must be distinguished from the hundreds of cities that are located on often just a few global circuits; while these cities are articulated with the global economy, they lack the mix of resources to manage and service the global operations of firms and markets.[22]

The world city concept became an extremely popular way of thinking about cities in globalization, and gained a clear quantitative foundation through Peter Taylor's (2004) idea of a relational "world city network" and through Sassen's work on intracity firms (box 5-1). A major strand of research became focused on how the global cities system was reshaping social life, while other researchers sought to craft quantitative schemes for measuring city powers and networks. Yet there continued to be a shared presumption that certain elite cities exercised near monopoly control, a position that has sometimes been overstated. Some of the empirical claims remain unsubstantiated and are still being elaborated. One repeated concern is that the role of financial services to global cities has been exaggerated or misinterpreted.[23]

*The Third Phase*

In the past decade, beginning in about 2007, a third direction of analysis has come to the fore that rejects the idea that just a few cities have command-and-control clout over the fates of other cities and the global system as a whole. The rise of emerging markets has illustrated a growing number of "ordinary" cities with globally relevant characteristics and assets.[24] Thus, attention has turned away from finance and toward industries such as fashion, the creative industries, and tourism, whose leading cities have a very different profile. Indeed, many analysts have noted

---

### BOX 5-1.  GLOBALIZATION AND WORLD CITIES (GAWC)

The research group Globalization and World Cities, founded at Loughborough University, has been responsible for many break-through theoretical and analytical understandings of global cities. One of its major contributions is a measure of global city networks that categorizes cities by the degree of global connectivity in their advanced services economies. The GaWC's measure has come to signify what it means to be a bona fide global city, high-lighting the importance of cooperation within networks rather than competition for capital and knowledge.

Since 2000 the *World According to GaWC* has provided figures every two or four years for comparative density of business firm office networks (accountancy, advertising, law, management consultancy, banking/finance and insurance). As more cities are analyzed, more cities are shown to be globally connected. In 2000 there were just sixty-eight Alpha and Beta (top-tier and second-tier) cities; now there are more than 120. London and New York have remained the two elite cities in the GaWC matrix since the start, closely followed by Hong Kong. But the progress of Shanghai, Beijing, and Dubai is very noticeable over time, as is, at lower levels of intensity, that of Shenzhen, Guangzhou, Hanoi, Cape Town, Lagos, and Lima.

---

that even the cities considered to be global financial leaders have seen employment in the sector shrink in recent years while employment in other sectors has soared.[25]

Some prominent thinkers in this most recent phase of conceptual development believe that the original notion of global cities was mired in conceptual incoherence and has been made more complex by the attempts of lower-rung cities to position themselves as global or international in some way. While not trying to pin down the exact nature of the global city, analysts of this disposition tend to share at least a few basic presuppositions:

- Many more cities are becoming globalized, more so than was previously recognized, and moreover, many have been globally oriented from very early on in their history, having accumulated rich assets and advantages.
- Global cities are part of broader geographic regions with complex labor markets and social cleavages.
- Global cities are centers of culture, learning, creativity, and innovation.
- Through their networks and diplomacy, global cities have a degree of agility to solve the entrenched problems their national and supranational governments cannot or will not solve.
- An increasing tension is visible between cities and their nation-states or national societies, and this tension will loom large over the next few decades.

THE EMERGING SCIENCE OF CITIES    Alongside this third wave there has been a major surge in attention directed toward the performance of global cities and their future prospects. The opportunities for and threats posed to individual global cities and systems of cities have begun to be identified in a more consistent way. The impact of the global financial crisis and the increased pace of economic change since 2008 have eliminated complacency about the future competitiveness of global cities, especially those in Europe and North America. Consistent weaknesses in the efforts of higher tiers of government to provide growing cities with the investment and fiscal tools they need to manage expansion and finance development have also triggered new directions of thinking and advocacy.

Regional and global institutions such as the World Bank, the Organization for Economic Cooperation and Development (OECD), the UN, and other international financial institutions have become thought leaders on the meaning and opportunity of global cities because of their cumulative experience advising or supplying capital to numerous cities over the past fifty years.[26] Their engagement is motivated by a recognition that global cities have the ability to drive change on growth and development issues. A body of work has therefore been built up that is supported and refined by academia, private corporations, research foundations, philanthropies, and citizen groups.

Several landmark studies beginning in the 1990s have informed the new approach to defining and comparing global cities. In the 1990s, in the hiatus without metropolitan government and while recovering from a recession, London was the source of much thought leadership in this arena. After the 1991 *London: World City* report asserted a new agenda of global competition, the 1996 study *Four World Cities: A Comparative Study of London, Paris, New York and Tokyo* built an influential evidence base.[27] Commissioned by the then Government Office for London, it was one of the first reports to articulate London's competition in globally traded sectors.[28] It also proposed that global cities should prioritize the state of the physical fabric of the inner city, the quality of amenities, transport links, the regulatory framework, and city image and marketing.

Global institutions were also prominent in this early stage of reviewing the future of global cities. For more than twenty years the OECD has been at the leading edge of urban thinking. In 1994, Melbourne hosted the OECD-Australia conference, "Cities and the New Global Economy," in one of the world's largest ever gatherings on urban policy. The ideas put forward led to a series of Territorial Reviews—diagnoses and evaluations of metropolitan area competitiveness worldwide. These were later summarized in the OECD's 2006 report, *Competitive Cities in the Global Economy,* which identified a global "common market of metropolitan economies."[29] The OECD noticed that the larger metropolitan area economies tended to outperform their nation-states, but that competition from other cities was becoming intense. The report has been influential in encouraging city and metropolitan area leaders to focus on increasing innovation, broadening cultural diversity, improving infrastructure, and applying rational metro governance. All of these areas have become core parts of the agenda of governments at all levels working to support global cities.

Alongside the work conducted on global cities, substantial effort has gone into understanding the major trends of the world's cities more generally, led especially by international financial and development institutions. UN-Habitat's *The State of the World's Cities* series, launched in 2001, has advocated for national governments to help solve housing, social, and environmental problems and let cities thrive as an interface between local and global economies, with a sharper lens turned toward productivity in cities.[30] And the World Bank's groundbreaking *World Development Report 2009: Reshaping*

*Economic Geography* was influential in crystallizing new thinking on cities and globalization. The latter has driven consensus that cities are the main vehicle through which to bring about economic development and observed that economic activity concentrates not just in cities but in higher-density areas within them that can support specialized clusters with global connections. The report also popularized the idea of systems of cities, which arise when cities build complementary specializations in national or regional systems.

This initial thinking has been fleshed out and updated recently by the McKinsey Global Institute, the World Economic Forum's work on city competitiveness, and the World Bank's 2015 review of competitiveness in cities. In addition to this body of investigation, there are more than 200 benchmarks and indexes that now have a global cities focus, created by consultancies, university departments, and advocates from within cities. Prominent examples of these studies include the following:

- 2thinknow Consulting: *Innovation Cities Global Index*
- A.T. Kearney: *Global Cities Index*
- CASS (Chinese Academy of Social Sciences): *Global Urban Competitiveness Project*
- Economist Intelligence Unit (EIU): *Hot Spots- Benchmarking Global City Competitiveness*
- EIU: *Global Liveability Ranking* (by year)
- fDi Magazine: *Global Cities of the Future*
- IBM: *The World's Most Competitive Cities*
- IBM: *Global Location Trends*
- Jones Lang LaSalle: *JLL Global 300*

- KPMG/Paris Investment Agency: *Global Cities Investment Monitor*
- Martin Prosperity Institute: *Creative and Diverse: Ranking Global Cities*
- Mori Memorial Foundation: *Global Power City Index*
- National University of Singapore: *Global Liveable Cities Index*
- Z/Yen Group: Global Financial Centres Index
- Saffron Brand Consultants: *The World City Business Brand Barometer*
- Savills: *World Cities Review*
- Toronto Regional Board of Trade: *Toronto as a Global City: Scorecard on Prosperity*
- UN-Habitat: *State of the World's Cities-City Prosperity Index*
- Xinhua-*Dow Jones: International Financial Centers Development Index*

## DEFINING CITIES UNDERGOING GLOBALIZATION: WORLD CITIES, MEGACITIES, GLOBAL CITIES, MEGALOPOLISES

Despite the conceptual development that has occurred in recent waves of globalization, global cities are still poorly understood, and there is no agreed-upon definition of what makes a city global (box 5-2). Especially in recent years there has been a reluctance to propose a single clear and comprehensive definition. The academic literature has tended to define a global city as one that is a key center for the high-value traded producer services economy. But there are also examples of global cities described as simply the very largest city economies, or the group of cities with the largest throughput of people and goods at their airports

"[A global city is] one which successfully competes for major city status in at least one of the several important functions of integrating the transntional capitalist economy in a neo-mercantilist world."
—Ann Markusen and Vicky Gwiasda, University of Minnesota, Humphrey School of Public Affairs, 1994

"World cities [are] particular 'postindustrial production sites' where innovations in corporate services and finance have been integral to the recent restructuring of the world-economy now widely known as globalization."
—Jonathan Beaverstock (University of Bristol), Richard. G. Smith (Swansea University), Peter J. Taylor (Northumbria University), 1999

"[Global cities are] major nodes in the organization of the world economy: hubs of economic control, production and trade, of information circulation and cultural transmission, and of political power."
—Derek Gregory (University of British Colombia), Ron Johnston (University of Bristol), Geraldine Pratt (University of British Columbia), Michael Watts (University of California, Berkeley) and Sarah Whatmore (University of Oxford), 2009

"Globalizing cities are both global cities seeking to maintain their position and non-global cities seeking to become global cities."
—John Rennie Short (University of Maryland, Baltimore), 2004

"Global cities around the world are the terrain where a multiplicity of globalization processes assume concrete, localized forms. These localized forms are, in good part, what globalization is about. . . . Most of today's major global cities are also world cities, but that there may well be some global cities today that are not world cities in the full, rich sense of that term."
—Saskia Sassen (Columbia University), 2005

"Global cities are simply whatever we as researchers define global cities to be."
—James Tyner (Kent State University), 2006

and ports. Also extant in the literature are definitions that include cultural influence and factor in elements such as language, media, diversity, and cultural assets.

Because of this lack of clarity and agreement, there is still uncertainty about how many global cities exist. At the most exclusive end are estimates of fewer than twenty genuinely global command-and-control cities. In the middle range, a 2015 Chicago Council on Global Affairs review estimated "40 or 50" cities with the qualities to be global.[31] Others have identified more than 100 global cities, while still others implicitly consider at least 300 cities to have globally traded functions.[32]

One reason for the lack of agreement on what makes a global city lies in the competing ideas about what constitutes globalness. Another is the lack of a harmonized approach to describing city size, geography, and the settlement system. At least three different variables are evident in the descriptions of global cities: globalness, significance, and organization.

**Globalness.** A city's globalness refers to the global or international dimensions of the city's economy, institutions, and society. Some assessments evaluate globalness simply according to the amount of foreign investment, the strength of international tourism, or the degree of population diversity. Taken individually, these figures may be misleading and may not reflect the city's success in tradable sectors or its global ties and reach.

**Significance.** A city's significance generally refers to its size and importance in national and regional contexts. Cities that are very large population centers are sometimes called global because of their presumed influence and diversity, as are capital cities or cities at the top of their domestic urban hierarchy, with decisionmaking and diplomacy functions. However, by other measures some of the most global cities in the world have fewer than 3 million inhabitants (for example, Dubai and Zurich), while many 10-million-person megacities (say, Lagos) have economies with quite limited international or transcontinental orientation.

**Organization.** City organization refers to the governance apparatus and to a city's fit with its functional geography. Global cities are usually wider metropolitan entities with a physically contiguous urban area and an integrated labor market. In geographic terms, global cities function as urban agglomerations. Often the terms *city region* or *global city region* are used to capture urbanization at a metropolitan or larger scale. Other terms in common use include gateway cities, megacities, metacities, supercities, megalopolises, megaregions, and polycentric metropolises, all of which try to grasp how urban form has been stretched and reshaped by economic and technological change. The different terms used to describe global cities often conflate factors of function, scale, spatial form, and level of development.

Because of the many interpretations of globalness, size, and organization that become apparent in debates about global cities, one thing is clear: there is no ultimate watertight definition that captures every dimension of cities at the leading edge of globalization. Definitions have evolved over time as new aspects of cities have come to the fore—from their wealth and power, to their mixed populations, to their financial services activities, to their changing spatial form, to their brand, identity, or soft power. We can expect future definitions to draw on aspects that are only just becoming visible now. These may include the changing role of nation-states and of business in global cities, which are new and important arenas of exploration.[33] It is also likely that future definitions will incorporate the challenges global cities face and the effectiveness of their response much more than current definitions do. Despite the increasingly rich histories of global cities that are available, it is contemporary experience that often brings the hurdles and difficulties associated with the global city model into full focus. These challenges are explored more fully in chapter 7.

## MEASURING GLOBAL CITIES: COMPARATIVE BENCHMARKING

Given the complexity involved in defining global cities, some have turned their attention to measuring performance instead. As mentioned above, many comparative benchmarking studies have been undertaken in the past decade to assess changing processes and priorities for cities.

The urge to compare cities is very strong in the current cycle, and a number of world-leading organizations have set the tone when it comes to benchmarking cities. UN-Habitat's City Prosperity Index provides baseline information to form the basis for long-term evidence-based policies, especially on social inclusion and basic infrastructure.[34] The Brookings Institution's Global Metro Monitor has become the leading barometer of the health of metro economies worldwide, offering deep insight into the changing patterns of growth and the fortunes of emerging global cities. And McKinsey's research arm, the McKinsey Global Institute, has produced a number of global comparative studies, as well as Cityscope, a global database of more than 2,000 cities designed to aid policymakers and businesses. Together, these studies offer a lens not only on comparative performance but also on wider trends such as the rise of medium-sized cities and the role of leadership in delivering adequate infrastructure investment.

## Indexes of Global Cities

Alongside the leading global indexes, in 2016 there are now more than 200 city indexes, rankings, and benchmarking reports comparing city performance. This figure is on the rise, up from fewer than 100 in 2011. City indexes are devised and sponsored by all kinds of public and private sector bodies, from international institutions to business consultancies, research foundations, industry specialists, news organizations, media outlets, and many more.

The field of city indexes is fast changing and reflects the work of both thoughtful research initiatives and more opportunistic businesses and organizations. Several established companies and consultancies work alone to produce high-profile indexes, while others are created by partnerships between universities, foundations, city governments, and businesses. Many draw on well-established data sets; others use real-time data and big data to observe city complexity. The industry of city indexes is becoming more global, with growing participation from organizations in Asia and, increasingly, Latin America and sub-Saharan Africa.

With more than 200 indexes in circulation, global cities are now compared not just on business and investment performance. Quality of life, reputation and influence, infrastructure platforms, cultural amenities, knowledge assets, innovation potential, and resilience are all the subjects of objective and perception-based studies. Many such measures have become well known and are of great interest to city leaders seeking to benchmark their own progress and make the internal case for reform.

A number of indexes stand out for their quality, influence, or comprehensiveness (box 5-3). From the more than 200 indexes available, there are several areas in which global cities are being more frequently compared:

**Livability.** The indexes highlight the fact that many leading global cities are experiencing deficits in infrastructure, housing supply, and employment that make them relatively less affordable and inclusive places to live. Smaller Central European and Canadian cities appear to have a more secure model. However, there are still widespread objections that indexes in this area suffer from anecdotalism, a bias toward Western cities, and incomplete geographic coverage.

**The innovation economy.** The innovation economy is a major area of comparative study as global cities seek to capture the opportunities associated with startups and digital technology. Indexes evaluating this dimension have emphasized the rapid emergence of cities such as Austin, Texas, and Amsterdam because they have been able to create the conditions for younger workers to move in and settle. Indexes are now starting to compare global cities

BOX 5-3. SIX OF THE LEADING CITY INDEXES

CASS GLOBAL URBAN COMPETITIVENESS PROJECT. One of the first major indexes was constructed by the Global Urban Competitiveness Project, a unique collaborative effort between universities, mostly in China, the United States, and Europe. A vast amount of data was collected by Chinese graduate students to inform the index, and the project defined city competitiveness in terms of productivity and corporate performance. The reports have measured the competitiveness of 500 cities across nine indicators, moving increasingly from hard factors toward factors such as innovation and creativity. North American cities have performed very strongly, with Chicago and Los Angeles ranking higher on this index than on almost any other. The project's authors have argued that the gap between the best and the worst is widening and that city promotion, metropolitan integration, and support for small businesses are critical.

A.T. KEARNEY GLOBAL CITIES INDEX. A.T. Kearney, another first-mover, has published the Global Cities Index since 2008 as a supplement to its country-focused Globalization Index. It has been one of the most widely publicized and authoritative indexes because of its comprehensiveness and its distinctive definition. Unlike some other indexes it does not just focus on business concentration and the breadth and depth of human capital. It also weighs the ability of cities to communicate and influence through media, newspapers, and the internet and it evaluates the degree of political representation and leverage it has. The premise is that cross-border influence rather than sheer scale has emerged as the decisive indicator of success. The index highlights the importance for cities to build networks and institutions that keep them engaged and relevant.

**GLOBAL POWER CITY INDEX.** First devised by Japan's Institute for Urban Strategies and the Mori Memorial Foundation, the Global Power City Index (GPCI) is one of the most rigorous examinations of the urban system, incorporating contributions from world leading urban academics and analysts. The GPCI has provided a valuable benchmarking tool for Tokyo and has highlighted the importance of R&D, environmental assets, and the intangible qualities cities offer to residents and visitors. The index also breaks down cities' appeal to different types of "customer," including managers and artists. The focus on functionality and sustainability in its methodology sees smaller European cities continue to excel, while Seoul has been the biggest improver inside the top ten.

**CITIES IN MOTION.** Published for the first time in 2014, the IESE Cities in Motion index added a new perspective by highlighting the importance of urban planning, public management, technology and social cohesion. The index observes that the quality of planning and leadership in global cities is vital if they are to become more efficient and sustainable. Mature global cities perform very strongly because of their improved city leaderships, world-class talent pools, and investments in technology.

**GLOBAL CITIES SURVEY.** Indexes intended for property investors have been an important feature of city rankings. Knight Frank's Global Cities Survey has been one that tried to offer a rounded assessment of locations based on what affects decisions made by wealthy and influential property owners. Again, political influence and intellectual activity were prominent in the methodology because global cities are said to need a "broad base of appeal . . .

Continued

[and] where the ideas and values that define the global agenda and shape the world are settled."

Agencies within a global city also create influential indexes that specifically track the performance of their home city. The Toronto Regional Board of Trade's Scorecard on Prosperity examines twenty-four cities and highlights the importance of good transport mobility and the livability to attract talent. Leading cities consistently in this study include Paris, Calgary, and Oslo.

on their policy and ecosystem frameworks for innovation, although a lack of reliable data on Asian and African innovation cities makes it difficult to assess the global geography of entrepreneurship.

**Sustainability and resilience.** The sustainability and resilience of global cities is now an established theme in the field of city indexes. After some years when comparative data proved hard to come by, organizations are creating new ways of comparing cities' policies, air pollution levels, infrastructure durability, and resource efficiency. The work of the British engineering firm Arup and the C40 Global Cities network has been one driver of comparative evaluation. In 2016 the impact of sensor technologies and mobile phone apps is thought to offer a route to a more accurate comparison of cities' sustainability.

**Reputation and influence.** Index compilers try to survey public opinion and the attitudes of decisionmakers to capture and compare the elusive dimension of city image. The more mature global cities tend to have enduring brands, even when their economies flounder. But indexes also help emerging cities see how far behind they are and can prompt small globalizing cities to evaluate their tourism and business brands.

It should be clear from this brief list that international comparative city indexes span a vast range of topics. However, a number of dimensions are not addressed by these indexes because of conceptual and data deficits.

Perhaps most important, there are almost no comparative measures on city governance, whether in terms of fiscal capacity, quality, or strength of city leadership, and the institutional framework, including at the metro level. These issues are seen as critical for global cities, but a comparative conceptual framework to measure performance across cities is still missing.

Other lacunae include the lack of comparisons of spatial development and housing supply relative to demand, and strategies linked to density. There has also been a surprising lack of comparative work done on social and economic inclusion, cultural diversity and interaction, relationships between groups or systems of cities, and global cities' capacity to generate investment returns. There is an imperative for progress to be made in these areas.

SUMMARY   Global cities have been the subject of intellectual inquiry for a century, and this scrutiny has intensified in the past twenty-five years. Because analysts work with different political and theoretical assumptions, there remains no agreed-upon framework for understanding the concept of a global city. But there is broad agreement that more cities are globalizing and that the time frames and economic pathways of such globalization are more richly varied than was previously recognized. The growth of city indexes, which are still in their infancy, is likely to continue in the coming cycles of globalization, with the indexes becoming more refined and more sensitive to differences.

# SIX GLOBAL CITIES TODAY

THE CURRENT WAVE OF global urbanization, beginning in 2008, exhibits the coincidence of three different types of global cities (figure 6-1). One type consists of *established global cities,* such as London, New York, Tokyo, and their peers, which were the dominant global cities of the past thirty to fifty years and today are corporate hubs, financial centres, and often capital cities. In a second group are *emerging global cities,* such as Istanbul, São Paulo, Shanghai, and their peers, which are the largest cities in the fastest-growing and most rapidly globalizing economies. These cities play important roles in connecting their nations into global flows and networks. The third group comprises what might be called *new global cities*, such as Brisbane, Cape Town, Oslo, San Diego, Santiago de Chile, Tel Aviv, and their peers. These cities are smaller, highly livable cities specializing in the newly globalizing sectors,

FIGURE 6-1.  TYPES OF GLOBAL CITY IN THE CURRENT CYCLE OF GLOBALIZATION (SINCE 2008–09)

ESTABLISHED
GLOBAL CITIES

EMERGING
GLOBAL CITIES

NEW
GLOBAL CITIES

High quality
of life cities

Port and
airport cities

Knowledge hubs

New gateway
cities

Specialized
centers

Visitor
destinations

Re-emerging
capital cities

led by life sciences, digital technologies, convergence technologies, and traded urban services.

In addition to these three core groups, several other types of globalizing city exist, reflecting the many different ways that cities are now participating in the global economy (see box 6-1). We may think of Auckland as a high-quality-of-life city, Busan as a port city, or Bangkok as a visitor destination city, but all are on a journey toward becoming global cities integrated into a much larger network. Over time, as these cities in other categories become more intentional, strategic, and diversified, they have tended to resemble cities in one of the three core groups.

ESTABLISHED GLOBAL CITIES   The many ways in which cities are measured (see chapter 5) highlight a small, elite cluster of uniquely globalized cities with their own set of specific assets and challenges. Cities in this group have been positioned for global trade and opportunity for at least three business cycles dating back to the 1960s, if not many more. Because of their mature clusters, business in these cities is usually conducted in several languages, in multiple currencies, and across several time zones. What is distinct about the cities in this group is that they have the concentration of transnational corporate firms combined with the service and infrastructure platforms and the cultural appeal to achieve genuine global reach.

With respect to these qualities, six cities continue to stand out: London, New York, Paris, and Tokyo, recently joined by Hong Kong and Singapore. This group has been described as the "command-and-control" centers of the world economy (box 6-1). That conceptual frame is somewhat outdated as new forms of metropolitan power, influence, and success have emerged. But these established global centers continue to have unique competitive assets and a unique attraction to capital owing to their political stability, labor pools, legal and regulatory frameworks, and institutional professionalism. Each is now developing its business model to integrate new technologies and new markets.

Of course, this group of cities is not a closed shop, and there is competition from cities that have invested more

BOX 6-1.  NEW YORK: WHERE THE WORLD DOES BUSINESS

New York is an established global city that draws on 100 years of uninterrupted global leadership. It effectively assumed the position of global financial capital after 1918 as it bankrolled a shattered Europe (and did so again in 1945). Even as New York's manufacturing sector declined in the 1960s and 1970s, it quickly adapted to a new world order. As American and other global firms moved production facilities south or abroad, finance, information services, management consultancy, and legal services consolidated in New York. Its accumulated expertise and a new generation of entrepreneurs made New York one of the coordinators of the new geography of trade. Successive outward-looking mayors worked hard to support these new activities and attract global firms, unlocking new waves of investment to reverse urban insecurity and decline and draw talent back to New York.

rapidly in upgraded infrastructure and connectivity. Their leadership may be seen as vulnerable to younger cities that can learn from their mistakes and capture the spillovers from excess demand. The most obvious candidates to join the six preeminent world leaders are Seoul, Toronto, and Sydney, which have acquired some of the financial, headquarter, and institutional critical mass, and offer important livability advantages.

At the same time, these established cities' size and success, pace of growth, and demand from new populations, investors, and enterprises are attended by a particular set of negative externalities, including congestion, inflation, environmental problems, inadequate housing supply, and two-speed economies in which the lower-

Today the wider New York metro area is home to more than 20 million people and is America's largest metro exporter ($127 billion worth of goods and services in 2014). In addition to its leadership in the corporate world, it has used its phenomenal concentration of talented young people and globally oriented firms, as well as its cultural image, to become a leader in art, media, fashion, film, digital, and cultural industries. Successive mayors have fought to keep the city open and supportive to immigrants, while since 2008 massive investments in the tech sector now make New York a truly diversified global city, a master of all trades.

Note: This phrase "Where the World Does Business" is a registered trademark of the New York City Economic Development Corporation.

and middle-skilled are unable to access good jobs or to afford good housing.

Because of institutional inertia, improvements in these cities are complex, incremental, and costly. In the centralized nations there is a strong reliance on national governments to help deliver some of the reforms that will address these deficits, such as fiscal devolution and investment in London, business-friendly zones in Tokyo, and regional infrastructure and innovation platforms in Paris.

In the more devolved countries there is a desire to shift toward a higher investment and better coordination equilibrium, for example with airport investment in New York. In the autonomous and semiautonomous cities of Singapore and Hong Kong, the larger issue is how to accommodate growth successfully given their land constraints.

### EMERGING GLOBAL CITIES

In the fastest-growing and larger economies, the big cities and the capital cities are becoming gateways and engines of international economic activity. In the current wave of globalization, since 2008–09, these cities are becoming bona fide world cities. Today, of the 100 most globalized cities (according to the Globalization and World Cities research group), nearly half are middle-income and lower-income cities.[1] At the same time, more than a quarter of firms with revenue above U.S. $1 billion are now based in emerging cities.[2] As a result, the economic performance of emerging cities is becoming much more closely indexed to global demand.

Emerging global cities are the business capitals of large domestic economies. Because of rapid and largely unmanaged growth in previous cycles, in the 1960s through the 1990s, when rapid deruralization in their nations turned many of them into megacities, they are experiencing many of the scale, governance, and implementation challenges of more established regions. However, the leading cities in each nation tend to be supported more actively by their national governments, which see them as gateways to global markets and capital. Most are in a dynamic process of economic adjustment and metro restructuring to optimize the benefits of global engagement.

The traded specializations in the emerging cities vary. Some, such as Shanghai, Shenzhen, Riyadh, and Taipei, specialize in financial services and attendant business services. Others, especially in East Asia, depend heavily on their hardware and engineering capacity. Then there are the regional centers of asset management, real estate, and R&D, such as São Paulo and Moscow. There are also the strategically located hubs for logistics and tourism, such as Istanbul.

Emerging global cities are not all at the same stage. Shanghai and Beijing are in the vanguard of this group, having gained major global roles and functions, with strong urban management tools (figure 6-2). They are already beginning to transfer lower-value industries and nonspecialist activities to neighboring cities and suburbs. Elsewhere is a group of cities comprising major emerging investment gateways that have an impressive infrastructure project pipeline, which augurs well for their capacity to absorb growth at a metro scale. Kuala Lumpur, Taipei, Istanbul, Buenos Aires, and São Paulo are examples, but these cities have bigger quality-of-life, infrastructure, and governance rigidities (box 6-2).

Many other cities may also be categorized as emerging global cities but are still low-wage economies and face even more acute infrastructure supply challenges. For Mumbai, Manila, and Jakarta, global city aspirations are visible but are constrained by leadership, governance, and coordination issues that make preparing, assembling, and executing projects much more complex than for the emerging global cities highlighted above. Finally, there are the emerging megacities with some international dynamics but that are not fully integrated into global value chains and have huge issues connected to

FIGURE 6-2.  SHANGHAI: EMERGING GLOBAL CITY

Source: Glas Jannes, *Shanghai: A Panorama View of Riverside of Pudong.*

youth unemployment and lack of consumer demand. For cities such as Dhaka and Lagos, fundamental issues of local capacity and political stability are preconditions for a more accelerated phase of globalization.

These groupings suggest that the rise of emerging global cities is not a monolithic process. Some are globalizing strongly in the current wave, while others may not be in a position to do so fully until future cycles. Often their performance is closely linked to their capacity to invest in growth through revenue generation, their readiness for the private sector, and their ability to partner with the national government. Many face the dilemmas that more established global cities first tried to address fifty years

## BOX 6-2. ISTANBUL: BACK TO THE FUTURE WITH EUROPE'S NEWEST GLOBAL CITY

Istanbul is regaining its global influence, and is today an emerging global city. Its return to prominence began when nationalist leadership focused on industrial investment in the 1950s, triggering very rapid population growth and a growing consumer class. In the 1980s, following a military coup, liberalization of Turkey's economy opened the city up to foreign investment. The city became a regional industrial and financial services hub, and the creation of a metropolitan municipality in 1984 allowed the city to start steering its own growth.

Spurred on by improved access to European and ex-Soviet markets, Istanbul's and Turkey's leadership deliberately sought to transform Istanbul into a global centre. Major housing and infrastructure investment was initiated, and gradually the city's finance, logistics, and tourism demand began to grow. Today, with the city among the top ten most visited worldwide, a third airport is under construction, as is a third Bosphorus bridge, as well as major road and rail connections. Ground is being broken for a new Istanbul Finance Centre, while the city is starting to support technology startups and initiatives. The city has actively played host to numerous conferences and festivals, culminating in its title of 2010 European Capital of Culture. Istanbul is now a major headquarters hub for European firms looking east, and Turkish firms looking to the former USSR, where they play important roles in real estate, finance, and architecture.

ago—how to avoid or reduce car dependence, where to build to cope with demographic strain and achieve a new multicentered structure, and how to address environmental problems to make the city more livable.

**NEW GLOBAL CITIES** The current wave of globalization, since 2008–09, has seen the rise of many smaller, more specialized, but highly globally oriented cities. Cities in this group are neither established nor emerging. They are smaller, high-income and high-livability cities, with efficient infrastructure and fewer social or environmental risks such as terrorism, air pollution, vehicle congestion, unaffordability, or inequality. Unlike emerging or established global cities, they often are not the primary city in their national or regional system of cities.

These new global cities have begun to internationalize their economies based on a small number of specializations derived from their comparative advantages as smaller, more livable, and attractive centers. Several are knowledge, cultural, or entertainment hubs, but many also possess high-tech, innovation, science, or research capabilities that make them important cities in the convention and higher education economies.

Because they rarely have important political or institutional functions, new global cities have a certain agility to shape their destiny, and compete to become recognized destinations for talent, events, and innovation.

Several drivers have given rise to new global cities: the changing center of economic gravity, the rapid expansion in size and mobility of the global middle class, the inability of the biggest cities to absorb demand, and technology's disruption of older production, integration, and consumption models. The new global cities are also able to compete for a larger number of globally traded sectors—especially digital media, urban services, entertainment, and life sciences—which gives them the chance to hone a system for a specific model of globally focused growth. With more sectors now traded globally, cities are becoming global in different ways:

| | |
|---:|---|
| *Finance* | Dubai |
| *Digital technology* | Brisbane |
| *Trade* | Miami |
| *Diplomacy* | The Hague, Geneva |
| *Innovation* | Bangalore, Seattle |
| *Artistic creation* | Los Angeles |
| *Visitors* | Barcelona |
| *Institutions* | Washington, D.C. |

In this context, the new global cities are attracting a bigger share of global business and real estate investment. In many cases their platforms offer good value, an attractive regulatory climate, and the flexibility for multiple stages of business growth.[3] Of course, these advantages are not permanent, and it is likely that unanticipated consequences will become evident after one or two cycles of hosting globalized activity, as discussed below.

PATHWAYS TO BECOMING A GLOBAL CITY    The current wave of global and globalizing cities has brought into being a more diffuse typology of global cities. Cities leverage a much broader variety of assets and advantages in order to compete in the global economy and are also making internal changes, whether by building brand coalitions (Stockholm), adapting metropolitan governance (Sydney), or investing in infrastructure platforms (Dubai).

Thus, although the first-mover cities still have big advantages, the assets and tactics that matter are more evenly distributed among cities of diverse size, offerings, and position on the globalizing trajectory. Many more metropolitan areas than in the past are able to plot their own course and develop global reach. This raises the question of which path a city should adopt, in light of the factors—trade, entrepreneurship, innovation, discovery, and geopolitics—that shape the global scene in any given cycle.

There are many different paths cities can take to become, first, globally aware, then more purposeful about their advantages, and finally to build an economic and governance system that is flexible and resilient to the externalities that will arise over time. At key points along the journey, leaders in the public and private sectors must grasp the global opportunity that awaits and recognize the need to build in more of the necessary ingredients for becoming a global city. Five distinct pathways that different cities have taken and that remain relevant today can be adduced.

## 1. Long-Term Trading Cities Accumulating Instincts to Globalize

As explored in chapters 2, 3, and 4, the history of cities participating in globalization shows that many first begin to operate as international trading hubs because of legacy factors favoring commercial exchange. The city economies that have been successful over the long term on this pathway have often achieved a high degree of independence in carrying out their commercial activity as part of self-conscious elite trading networks.

In the second phase of global orientation, the wealth and opportunities these cities offer make them popular places of refuge and immigration destinations when conflict, persecution, or disease afflict foreign groups. These cities inevitably acquire a reputation for being "safe havens" for merchants, entrepreneurs, intellectuals, bohemians, and capital. Their commercial disposition means they have business leadership groups that are well embedded in the city leadership structure and will urge a deliberate and strategic approach to global opportunities. A broad base of leadership helps ensure that connectivity infrastructure linking other cities—whether by sea, air, or rail—is upgraded regularly, often by using public investment surpluses.

After several cycles of development, immigration and investment, knowledge and innovation capacities come to the fore in these long-term trading cities, boosted by advanced higher education institutions and a commitment to freedom of thought. The increasingly international character of education, culture, and sport means the most globally fluent of these cities are able to forge compelling brand associations, usually linked to vibrancy, professionalism, and opportunity.

HAMBURG

Hamburg is a strong example of this kind of pathway. Its early advantages during the Hanseatic League era of globalization included strategic location, access to resources, political stability, and proximity to a network of other commercial centers. The city then achieved a precedent of a high degree of political autonomy. Although its independence has periodically been threatened by ambitious national leaders or during wartime, the wealth and power of the trading communities have ensured that commercial interests are not overridden for more than one political cycle.

After several centuries, Hamburg entered a qualitatively new phase when new kinds of production began to transform the economic system. Since the 1980s the city has been rigorous about securing its key assets, as evidenced by its expansion of port capacity. As a diverse trading city it has the variety of skills and the information needed to adjust to new human capital demands, working practices, and infrastructure and design needs. Its major HafenCity development stands out as one of Europe's leading waterfront projects, and the city's international building exhibition, IBA, has been an important precursor to outstanding innovation in the housing sector. Just as in the past, connectivity will be critical to Hamburg's future growth, and the city will need the Elbe to be dredged and the navigation channel widened to support large container ships in the China trade.

## 2. Opportunists of Geopolitical Catalysts

A number of globalizing cities have not always been the dominant economic power in their region but have subsequently profited from a conjunction of historical events. These events may include any of the following:

- the declining political fortunes of neighboring centers,
- sudden proximity or access to new booming markets,

- new opportunities to redevelop former imperial trade and population links, and
- abrupt changes in legal and regulatory climate preferences.

Favorable geographic and historical events usually have to be harnessed by regional alignment and national-level support. Political devolution, metro-wide government, federal initiative, and rational state engagement have all enabled cities benefiting from geopolitical opportunity to increase the rate of infrastructure investment and establish attractive tariff and sector policies.

For these opportunist cities, historical catalysts and an enabling government system create a platform to allow them to become more globally oriented. Two cities that fit this category, Singapore and Munich, are clear recent examples, demonstrating that an initial cycle of strategic government and market demand can result in the creation of targeted specializations, historically in fields such as advanced manufacturing, aerospace, and media.

A city taking this pathway needs to be able to secure investment for its economic priorities, whether through channeled state government funds or through the devolution of more metro-level financing powers. This helps these cities hold the edge in their logistics and transport platforms and attract talent and institutions in agile, fast-growing sectors. The role of the business community in these cities is important: leaders must be aware of global trends and work to develop influential leadership networks that promote a global outlook with respect to both exports and immigration.

Cities on this pathway may enter a third phase, by which point their initial advantages may be less obvious and new edges may be needed. These cities have usually diversified across R&D and services sectors and have established trading partners as a result of reliable air links and a large banking and insurance presence. The challenge is often to ensure the model of success can be coordinated at a wider metropolitan area scale, and to prevent those who benefited during the first cycle from locking out those who want to take part in the new cycle by preventing access to housing and opportunity.

## TORONTO

Toronto is distinctive for having leveraged a consensus about global economic positioning in order to become globally competitive during the post-1945 wave of rapid development and growth. Its global awareness hinged on the growing strategic relevance of its location, given its British Commonwealth links and migration, English-based legal systems, proximity to a growing U.S. market, and the flight from Montreal during the Francophone secessionist movement.

Toronto experienced a golden age in the 1980s thanks to housing and transport infrastructure investment that left a model of livability that has continued to draw new immigrants and tourists for several decades. It also has a mature culture of internationalist leadership that manages integration challenges intentionally. However, its global aspirations are not accompanied by investment tools to match, and Toronto's global city story is not yet complete.

## 3. Cities Leveraging Innovation

For some cities, the path to becoming a global city begins with their density of R&D, technology, tradable knowledge, skills, and innovation. They become the knowledge centers of their region either because of high-skill immigration, or because of the presence of major research institutes such as universities and hospitals, or because national governments choose to locate important military or scientific institutions there.

In a second phase, these cities, which are often smaller than the dominant cities in their national systems, gain experience while serving a domestic market or providing basic services for a small number of international companies, often led by returnees from larger commercial centers. The national and state governments, which may have paid these metro areas little attention, eventually begin to initiate programs of deregulation to improve the business climate and attract sector-specific foreign investment. Government also becomes more cooperative, easing regulations on international trade and aligning better with less restrictive political norms.

Several cities on this path have seen their business communities assume the lead with respect to the cities' strategy and positioning. It is common for the city to recognize the value of complementing its specialized economies with a stronger tourist and lifestyle proposition. Making itself appealing to graduates from around the country and the world is a big priority for a city in this group. Often one of the biggest challenges is weakness in governance and leadership arrangements, which may prevent these highly specialized metropolitan area economies from escaping domestic constraints.

NANJING

Nanjing has been a city of knowledge and commerce since the Ming dynasty. National public research institutes in aeronautics and military engineering were founded in the early 1950s. The city developed very strong electrical, mechanical, and steel specializations, but initially it had a reputation of not being business-friendly. But, as happened to Silicon Valley before it, a gradual, informal concentration of commercial practices and talent congregated, with or without deliberate state or national support, and with limited conscious local leadership. Expertise in the electronics sector clustered in Nanjing, and the city became famous for flat-panel TVs.

The impact of Ericsson, Volkswagen, and Sharp in Nanjing in the 1990s spurred a rapid increase in demand in the course of dynamic changes in technology industries. Thanks to its many science and technology institutions, Nanjing has been supplying large pools of talent to its software and science sectors, and the city has also tried to attract Chinese expatriates to return through its 321 Talent Plan. The city government has actively supported the push to innovation by investing in a biopharmaceutical innovation park and hosting international R&D summits. Nanjing is now well placed to be an education and research leader in the Asia-Pacific region as it enters its second cycle of global orientation.

## 4. *National Champion Cities*

Many cities around the world became globally oriented under the command of a central government, with a national policy for global engagement effectively dictating the city or metropolitan area strategy.

Often during periods of political or democratic transition, national leaderships have designated one or more of their cities as pioneers of global reform, and backed them with substantial public investment, support for hosting major events, and regulatory reform to encourage inward investment and global trade. Some of East Asia's most globalized cities began on this pathway; other examples include Moscow, Santiago de Chile, and most recently Colombo.

Being a national champion is a big advantage in terms of triggering a rapid phase of globalization and becoming a preferred recipient of domestic and international investment. But it is not an automatic recipe for long-term competitiveness. Rarely are these national projects set up with the main purpose of making the championed city more productive, livable, and sustainable. Rather, more often they have been designed as a way to promote the nation globally and burnish national prestige. Having a national champion may also mean that the city fails to gain significant self-governing autonomy as the national leadership seeks to retain direct control. Furthermore, national designation has often resulted in an unanticipated surge of rural in-migration, and later deep-seated deficits in services, infrastructure, and integration.

## SEOUL

Seoul began its global growth path when it became reestablished as Korea's undisputed growth engine during the country's administration by the United States and Ee Seung-man's presidency up until 1960. From a city of around 1 million people, Seoul grew very rapidly, and its economic structure transformed from a rural, agrarian system to that of a labor-intensive export hub, and later to an advanced industrial and postindustrial economy.

A regime of "state corporatism" that supported Korean industrial monopolies meant that large companies were invited to invest in particular industry sectors and were given access to cheap credit, facilitated by foreign aid. Such companies as Samsung (electronics) and Hyundai (vehicle and ship manufacturing) grew at an extraordinary pace. The family-run *jaebeol* corporation structure was able to respond quickly to market conditions. As the city was under the authority of the prime minister's office, the central government's firm economic and land development policies in the 1960s and 1970s helped Seoul build new infrastructure and prepare its labor force accordingly. This model was essential to Korea's growth all the way up to the time it hosted the 1988 Olympic Games, when Seoul was designated a "special city."

The national championing of Seoul has had lasting effects on the Korean system of cities. Although national policies subsequently tried to reassign growth to other regions, regulations ultimately failed to slow agglomeration in the capital region, and many of Korea's second cities have struggled to grow in recent decades. By 1997, the Seoul Metropolitan Readjustment Plan had recognized the region's role as South Korea's globally competitive hub, and the capital had its first directly elected mayor.[4]

This allowed Seoul to make progress with large-scale regeneration projects, most notably in Cheonggyecheon district, which has been redeveloped to support the city's transition toward creative and services industries. Even after the Asian financial crisis, the central government retained considerable oversight over Seoul's metropolitan government, and through its policy of *segyehwa*, Seoul opened up further to international trade, exchange, and investment. Today, as the city seeks to modernize, become more transparent, and transition to a higher-value economy, concessions from the central government are now sought to increase policy competences and reduce bureaucratic and financial inflexibilities inherent in the centralized government apparatus.[5]

## 5. Cities Given Momentum by International Events and Institutions

For some cities that are not highly globalized or that have stopped being globally oriented for some reason, international events or institutions can sometimes play an important catalytic role. They offer a way for newly globalizing (or reglobalizing) cities to raise their profile, accelerate infrastructure development, and become associated with particular ideas, values, or attractions. Global events such as Olympic Games and World Cup competitions have undoubtedly had a catalytic role for cities such as Barcelona, Turin, and Vancouver, but other events, both sporting and cultural, have helped raise confidence and ambition in cities and increased the capacity for hotels and business meetings. At the same time, the arrival of a recognized global institution, such as a supranational or nongovernmental headquarters, is also a catalyst for the clustering of global knowledge and expertise in a city, as has occurred in Nairobi since the arrival of the UN Environment Program in the 1970s, and also in Vienna and The Hague.

VIENNA

One of the great global cities of the eighteenth and nineteenth centuries, Vienna emerged from World War II having lost many of the qualities that made up its international character, including its Jewish and other populations, its intellectual buzz, and its avant-garde spirit. Its citizens were insular and sought homogeneity in the decades that followed. The establishment of Vienna as an East-West center for international diplomacy during the Cold War was the start of the city resuming its international role in the global economy.

With Austria a small state in an uncertain position in Central Europe in the 1960s, Foreign Minister Bruno Kreisky sought to pursue a policy of internationalization. After proposing Vienna as a host for international dispute resolution talks between the United States and the Soviet Union and between Israel and the Palestine Liberation Organization, Kreisky successfully attracted the United Nations to the city. Vienna offered itself as a home for the International Atomic Energy Agency and UNIDO, and a new set of buildings that become known as UNO City was built on land east of the historical city center. At the same time, Vienna successfully attracted OPEC to the city, ahead of Geneva, which was initially the favorite.[6]

This effectively established a new strand of Vienna's DNA. Since the construction of UNO City there has been a rapid expansion of the number of international organizations in Vienna. Several UN organizations relocated from New York, Geneva, and Beirut to make full use of the facility provided. Today more than 5,000 people from 110 countries work in UNO City, which has extraterritorial status.

Vienna's cluster of international institutions allowed it to positon itself at the geopolitical heart of Europe after the Iron Curtain came down. Vienna has benefited from its connections with the East, and has been able to resume cross-border business throughout the region. Credit growth in Central and Eastern Europe became highly interconnected with the fortunes of three Austrian banks based in Vienna, Raiffeisen Bank International, Erste Bank, and Bank Austria, and the Vienna Stock Exchange gained majority stakes in the bourses of Budapest, Prague, and Ljubljana. EU enlargement also encouraged flows of both people and investment, and Vienna has once again come to be seen as one of the most tolerant and culturally rich cities in the region. By 2005 the number of foreign-born residents in Vienna was almost three times higher than in 1980. Migrants today account for a majority of startup founders, many in IT, while there are more than 40,000 international students in the city.

SUMMARY    While there are distinct success models for different types of global cities, there also appear to be some common ingredients that mark out global cities:

- they support trade and specialization in traded sectors;
- they attract and retain entrepreneurial diverse populations;
- they foster innovation and achieve influence;
- they lead the discovery of new markets, routes, products, or services; and
- they take advantage of geopolitical opportunity.

In the twenty-first century, the imperatives to build, blend, and sustain these ingredients do not play out in the same way for each type of city. Different types of global cities have particular requirements associated with their roles and legacies that must be addressed if they are to achieve their goals.

*Established global cities* have experienced very high demand for forty years or more. When their leaders think about how to maintain their cities' momentum and avoid cycles of stasis or decline, they typically face three inter-related dilemmas: (1) how to manage and invest in growth, (2) how to maintain global leadership and specialization in prime sectors, and (3) how to resolve tensions with nation-states and upper-level authorities.

Because these cities are world leaders, with a huge appeal to talent and investment, many externalities connected with long-term demand and supply-side constraints have appeared. These include rising prices and inequality, a structural undersupply of housing, infrastructure systems in need of expansion and updating, and institutional formats that are a poor fit with new economic geographies. Without a growth management system, these cities risk population overload and property bubbles. Such a system needs new forms of investment, institutional reforms, and very active civic and business leadership. Each of these mandates is politically difficult to achieve.

While established global cities have become highly experienced at hosting corporate headquarters and advanced financial and professional services, many have now had to diversify their economies and make the business climate and ecosystems suitable both for new technology startups and for older banks and corporations. This highly nuanced activity requires fostering different kinds of business districts for distinct purposes while at the same time ensuring that the "old economy" and the "new economy" reinforce and support each other through trade, investment, and skills sharing. So the adaptability of established global cities to growth, new land uses, and a new generation of sectors and entrepreneurs is critical to their success.

Established global cities usually face a deep level of opposition within their nation-state or wider polity. They are often viewed as a cause of interregional disparities and the underlying reason for the failure of other, smaller cities. Consequently, a key task for these cities entails building a national narrative that supports their global roles and works to leverage their advantages nationally while mitigating the challenges that global leadership brings. The mix of strategic imperatives for this group of cities is shown in box 6-3.

*Emerging global cities* have capacity issues of a different kind. They need to solve three major barriers to growth and success: (1) finding flexible sources of investment for infrastructure and development; (2) attracting and developing talent and finding ways to bridge local skills gaps; and (3) organizing the metro space for the first time. Without systems and strategies to address these issues, emerging global cities will struggle to maintain their pace of economic development and to become preferred destinations for higher-value global activities (box 6-4).

BOX 6-3.  **STRATEGIC IMPERATIVES FOR MANY ESTABLISHED GLOBAL CITIES**

| | |
|---|---|
| *Population* | Prevent international in-migration from being cut off by higher tiers of government, limit out-migration of talent to cheaper cities. |
| *Housing* | Use multiple tactics to boost rate of supply. Confront tendency of property owners to oppose growth. |
| *Inequality* | Address urban exclusion through mix of social, spatial, and educational initiatives. |
| *Sustainability* | Catch up with leaders for climate change adaptation and resilience. |
| *Land* | Undertake big redevelopment efforts to shift from old to new modes and recycle land effectively. |
| *Business framework* | Maintain tax and business climate that supports both corporate and innovation economies. |
| *Talent* | Support talent to enter job market at appropriate levels. Maintain public support for openness nationally. |

Creating the right mix of incentives to attract and retain international and local talent and to improve capacity requires a careful mix of strategies. Without the combination of local and overseas talent, the longer sustainability and breadth of these cities' success may be at risk. Furthermore, most emerging global cities have not been through multiple cycles of institutional reform, as established global cities have. They have not yet created

| | |
|---|---|
| *Infrastructure* | Undertake bold infrastructure projects and smart integration, such as multimodal transport and smart water, waste, and energy policies. |
| *Economic development* | Ensure living and working costs are affordable for new entrants in the emerging innovation sectors. |
| *Brand and identity* | Maintain a clear and visible identity amid greater competition from globalizing cities. |
| *Metro governance* | Develop networked and collaborative governance across the functional region. Strengthen metro authorities without overcrowding the system. |
| *Intergovernmental relationships* | Improve fiscal arrangements with national government. Develop stronger relation-ships with second-tier cities to build the case for change. |

durable metropolitan governance, and they lack institutions with a depth of expertise in integrating growth management solutions that combine infrastructure build-out with land use, housing, and environmental concerns.

Because *new global cities* are smaller, they very quickly experience capacity constraints once they open up to international markets. They usually need to adapt their model of success in order to sustain their progress beyond the first initial cycle. This entails (1) achieving scale and visibility in globally traded sectors, (2) diversifying into

| BOX 6-4.   STRATEGIC IMPERATIVES FOR MANY EMERGING GLOBAL CITIES |

| | |
|---|---|
| *Population* | A more managed and transparent approach to population growth and to rural migration. |
| *Housing* | Provide attractive and sustainable entry-level housing at a pace and scale to match demand. |
| *Inequality* | Tackle forms of segregation and exclusion from accessing services. Roll out inclusive public transport to improve access to jobs. |
| *Sustainability* | Develop more robust strategies to cope with climate change, water shortages, flooding, earthquakes. |
| *Land* | Explore more effective use of prime urban land. Practice better spatial governance to achieve coherent urban and metro forms. |
| *Business framework* | Improve labor productivity and develop a stronger legal, tax, and regulatory framework. Focus on transparency and confidence. |

multiple sectors of leadership, and (3) retaining quality-of-life advantages after periods of population growth and change (box 6-5).

These cities have to achieve some global leadership in their chosen realms of specialization, where there is much competition. This involves both developing a keen understanding of their economic assets for advanced industries and also their ability to foster enterprise on a

| | |
|---|---|
| Talent | Maintain openness to international talent; foster cosmopolitanism and multilingualism. |
| Infrastructure | Promote rapid assembly of projects to address infrastructure and basic housing deficits. |
| Economic development | Provide greater support for new businesses and emerging innovation sectors adjacent to existing specializations. |
| Brand and identity | Establish a clear and compelling global identity, and live up to the brand promise. |
| Metro governance | Enhance municipal governments' capacity and tools, institutional maturity. |
| Intergovernmental relationships | Encourage recognition of metropolitan agenda and spatial economy by national government. Improve fiscal and incentive framework to avoid incentivizing sprawl and to capture the value of development. |

large enough scale to generate several clusters with global potential. Inevitably this involves prioritization, underwritten by a focused leadership and consistent decisionmaking.

There is a danger that new global cities will become seen as one-trick ponies, with only one aspect of their leadership visible (such as tourism in Barcelona, IT in Seattle, or clean tech in Copenhagen). There is also a risk

BOX 6-5.  STRATEGIC IMPERATIVES FOR NEW GLOBAL CITIES

| | |
|---|---|
| *Population* | Build alliances around talent attraction involving municipalities, universities, and business. |
| *Housing* | Monitor housing type and affordability to ensure good supply for younger workers and citizens. |
| *Inequality* | Focus strongly on inclusive growth via skills, sector partnerships, inner-city redevelopment, mixed-use housing. |
| *Sustainability* | Provide active leadership on energy efficiency and mix, low pollution, green economy, resilience. |
| *Land* | Develop agreed-upon spatial strategy to be managed by lead agency. Develop pipeline of projects with scale and deliverability to attract range of external investors. |
| *Business framework* | Improve information and coordination within and between sectors. Foster startup growth. |

that these cities will fail to live up to their brand promise because of the strains that appear across a full cycle of growth. Many newly global cities fall short in terms of their ability to host and scale innovation economy sectors, and surprisingly, many also struggle with road congestion and cost of living.[7]

As a result, many of their city and metro leadership organizations now work actively to limit the externalities

| | |
|---|---|
| *Talent* | Gain visibility among international talent and entrepreneurs; maintain affordability. |
| *Infrastructure* | Enhance international air and port links, especially to growth markets. Focus on digital connectivity. |
| *Economic development* | Introduce expert specialization, innovation, digital technology, science. Leverage big events, summits, and decisionmaking. |
| *Brand and identity* | Build a business and investor brand to complement city's other stronger brands. Maintain reputation for work-life balance. |
| *Metro governance* | Provide a broader leadership platform involving business, universities, and civil society. Embrace the metro agenda. |
| *Intergovernmental relationships* | Build the story from scratch and gain active support for internationalization program. |

that this demand places on their appeal and to create the conditions that will expand their innovation economy.[8] Projects such as the Greater Sydney Commission, the Barcelona Global Talent program, and the Project Oslo Region all reflect a new impetus to create the scale and maintain the quality needed to compete.

Global cities of all types, however, have in common a set of shared traits, behaviors, or characteristics, which they exhibit in different combinations. It is these assets that help explain how they can optimize global flows of capital, talent, trade and ideas. Some of these traits enable these cities to avoid becoming locked into negative path dependencies as circumstances change, as the unintended consequences of success manifest themselves, and as they enter new cycles. Chapter 7 turns to the future of global cities and takes up the leadership challenges they may face in greater detail.

# SEVEN THE FUTURE OF GLOBAL CITIES: CHALLENGES AND LEADERSHIP NEEDS

TODAY MORE ATTENTION THAN ever before is focused on how globalizing cities can prepare themselves to meet the challenges of the future. Of concern is not only the strategies and approaches of individual cities as they pursue a more global agenda. Serious national and regional assessments are also under way of the longer-term future of so-called systems of cities, in which globalizing cities combine with and influence the development of other cities in their region or nation, and the implications for future infrastructure and development between them.

This chapter considers what has been learned from this short history of global cities and looks ahead to the challenges global cities face and will face in the future. It identifies three challenges all cities will confront: (1) how to compete, (2) how to cope with success, and (3) how to build external partnerships. These challenges point up the vital role of leadership, and so the chapter concludes with reflections on how global cities can adjust their systems of leadership to better fit this urban age.

THE JOURNEY AHEAD FOR GLOBAL CITIES    The pace of change since 2008 is a sign of things to come. A new generation of global cities has rapidly emerged within the past decade, and some of these changes have affected the very top of the global system. The latest analysis from the McKinsey Global Institute suggests that by 2030, four of the top fifteen cities by absolute consumption will be emerging cities, namely, Beijing, Shanghai, Mexico City, and São Paulo.[1]

But the shift is much broader-based. The high costs of established global cities have created increased demand among mobile talent and investors for alternative locations in what were once thought of as second-, third-, or fourth-tier centers.

These new global cities are competing on their quality of place, lifestyle, open governance, and niche economic opportunities. Many have invested in urban transformation and workforce programs that have rapidly improved their prospects of becoming centers in the new innovation economy. The shift away from established global cities and toward both emerging and newly global cities, semidetached from trends in their national economy, is widely viewed as structural rather than cyclical.[2]

There are many reasons why the existing system of global cities is likely to change even more in the future. First, and most obvious, the number of cities with sufficient assets and population to "go global" is increasing all the time as global urbanization heads toward first 60 percent and then 70 percent. Already more than 500 urban areas have more than 1 million inhabitants. Another 100 more urban areas will join this list with every passing decade. Not all of these cities will have the ability or the appetite to go global, but diversification does mean that more cities on each continent are acquiring international functions and positioning their tradable sectors for global exchange.

Whereas twenty years ago there were perhaps only ten or fifteen global cities in each of the more advanced continental economies, there are now more than twenty-five global cities in each of Europe, North America, and Asia Pacific, and many other emerging global cities in Latin America and Africa.

The second reason why the global system of cities is set to expand has to do with disruptors. On the push side, twenty-first-century cities are expected to be profoundly affected by mass migration, climate change, terrorism, pandemics, environmental disasters, and resource conflicts. The force of these impacts will not be such as to propel people to relocate away from cities but rather will work to diversify the range of cities that grow and globalize.

So far, most of the global cities that have endured or are coping with these varied challenges (such as the 9/11 attacks and Hurricane Sandy in New York, the Fukushima nuclear disaster in Tokyo, and water shortages in Beijing) have managed to address the immediate crisis and take steps to improve resilience in their city systems. But the impact of future crises will likely reveal the inability of some cities to bounce back quickly and resume global operations. The vulnerability of global cities to some or all of these threats varies, but there is little doubt that these external disruptions will constrain some cities and serve to move a large number of others into more global roles.

There are also positive disruptors that are expected to change the landscape of global cities. The impacts of digital technology, big data, smart integrated systems, the sharing economy, the experience economy, and other innovations in production and consumption are already making themselves felt in cities. Many cities are becoming hubs for the new innovation economy (such as Austin, Nairobi, Oslo, and Shenzhen) and are developing ideas and solutions that have global traction and global reach. In many respects the disruptive innovations being produced in some of today's cities will be decisive in shaping the success of urbanization in the rest of the world.

The technological disruptors and the innovation districts in which they are produced, commercialized, and refined will ultimately provide opportunities for more cities to excel and export globally. At the same time, those cities that are slow to grasp the opportunity for smart densification, interoperable city systems, and real-time public services provision may find themselves becoming uncompetitive and even risking being locked into unproductive and unsustainable patterns of urbanization. "Smart city" and "future city" systems may prove to be enablers of growth and adaptation.

Just as it was in ancient and modern history, connectivity will also be a major driver of global cities in the future (box 7-1). Not only do connectivity platforms provide access to global markets but major infrastructure lines that connect regional clusters of cities and connected

## BOX 7-1.  THE NEW SILK ROAD: ONE BELT, ONE ROAD

Railway connections between Europe and Asia are the center-piece of a major geopolitical effort by China to establish a "New Silk Road" under the initiative called One Belt, One Road. Since 2011 a fully completed railway line has been used to convey freight between Chongqing, China, and Duisburg, Germany, within 13 days. Subsequently, Chinese leaders have sought to actively develop this line, which connects smaller cities such as Urumqi, Dostyk, Astana, Gomel, Brest, and Łódź.

This is just one dimension of a series of infrastructure partnerships, built around energy, telecommunications, logistics, legal systems, and IT, intended to serve overland and maritime Silk Roads connecting East and West. The goal of coordinating policy, connectivity, free trade, and the movement of capital across such a vast space is arguably unprecedented in its ambition. It allows cities not just in China but also in Iran, Pakistan, Sri Lanka, Turkey, the Gulf states, and elsewhere to build their own international platform and gain competitive advantage in a more Sino-centric economy.

city corridors are also set to become critical to cities' long-term growth and success, supported by coordinated metro and macro-regional planning and investment.[3]

Global cities as the nucleus of hyperconnected and cooperative city clusters are a growing trend, whether the city is Shanghai, the nucleus of the Yangtze River Delta; Manchester, the heart of the Northern Powerhouse; or Johannesburg, the hub of the Gauteng city region. The "functional federation" of cities across political borders, united by infrastructure and technology systems, is likely to become a major feature of global cities by the mid-twenty-first century.[4]

*Impacts for Global Cities*

What does this sea change in city functionality and connectivity mean for global cities? It is clear that becoming and remaining a global city involves addressing at least three broad types of challenge:

1. finding a path to compete and lead in a world that is rapidly globalizing and urbanizing,
2. tackling the consequences of success and growth within the city, and
3. dealing with and resolving external challenges to the global city model.

**LEARNING HOW TO COMPETE AND LEAD**  It is perhaps an obvious proposition that becoming a global city means learning how to be competitive and how to lead. To become the preferred location for mobile activities such as international trade, cross-border services, transnational firms, mobile merchants, entrepreneurs, migrants, and capital, and to foster the business climate, facilities, livability, and the logistics they need, is a deliberate task. It would be hard to get it right by accident. Even if an initial process of globalization is unintended or opportunistic, sustaining those global roles and functions over time requires an effort to remain one of the preferred locations, within a system of competition and contested choices.

The debate over what city competitiveness is ranges widely. Specific questions are frequently focused on the links between competitiveness and productivity, competitiveness and specialization (are specialized cities more competitive than diversified cities?), and short-run competitiveness (such as price competitiveness) versus longer-run competitiveness (such as value-added). There are also heated debates about the externalities and unintended consequences associated with competitiveness.

As recent studies by the World Bank and World Economic Forum show, there is no quick recipe for becoming a competitive city.[5] For economists, competitiveness is often equated with productivity. In the context of cities, productivity is the combined result of enterprise, innovation, skills, employment, investment, and the impact of competition on how these are encouraged. But for cities, competitiveness is about more than just productivity.

Coordination and promotion also play key roles because cities are different from businesses. They do not exist solely to support competitiveness and often have limited or unsuitable institutional frameworks, and their general reputations and identities may not emphasize their competitive assets. So competitiveness for cities involves attending to these governance issues, as well as to the drivers of productivity. Sustainability is also important for long-term city competitiveness. Without it, short-term efforts at competitiveness may be wasteful in the longer term.

Competitiveness is what allows cities to successfully enable their businesses and industries to trade, create jobs, drive innovation, raise productivity, attract investment, and build shared prosperity. Of course, in the context of cities, competitiveness also needs a public purpose. Being competitive is about increasing or protecting jobs, tax revenues, and investment in public goods, as well as enlarging or retaining key assets and population. Competitiveness is a means to secure resources that support social and environmental purposes. But there are big differences between cities, and these have an impact on their ability to achieve these public and longer-term goals.

This is not to say that all global cities are in competition with all other global cities all of the time and on all fronts. Indeed, the review in this book of how global cities evolve illustrates that there are now many distinct paths to globalization and that different kinds of global cities host varying functions.

Competition between global cities is an important dynamic, but it happens in specific and precise ways. Competition is widely regarded as potentially a spur to innovation and creativity as long as the competition is fair and not skewed by distorting forms of favoritism or the unwarranted advantaging of one city over another. This is one reason why the role of national governments is so important in many parts of the world. National governments can help their leading cities be more competitive in international contests, with net gains accruing to the national economy.

Some of the forms of intercity competition that can be observed follow.

■ **Between large and diverse leading cities on a continental and intercontinental level** There are occasional head-to-head competitions between the leading global cities, which otherwise exist within a framework of complementary functions according to continents and time zones. Thus, while London and New York and Hong Kong generally offer similar services but within different markets and coexist easily with one another, with a high degree of cooperation, there are occasional contests between them for the global headquarters of a financial institution, the first public listing of a growing global firm, or the location of a media and information services function.

■ **Between large, diverse cities and niche cities**   The same large and diversified cities also experience competition from smaller niche cities for specific functions in which they have a specialized competitive advantage and may combine this with advantageous business climate elements such as lower taxes or easier regulation. Thus the same cities of New York, Hong Kong, and London might also experience competition from Toronto and Miami, Dublin and Amsterdam, Kuala Lumpur and Taipei in niche activities such as specialized finance, technology and software, or asset management.

■ **Between niche cities**   There is a large and systematic set of competitions between smaller cities with specialized functions in the same sectors. Thus cities that specialize in computer games, mobile technology, life sciences, clean tech, media and information, and much more have no option but to compete for some of the same activities and assets that are helpful to growing their economies.

But for all these niche cities, the key to competition is building up their own indigenous strengths and assets, producing new firms and entrepreneurs and strengthening and leveraging their key economic assets (such as skills, universities, R&D facilities, and airports or the venture capital community, business schools, and large firms that anchor key clusters). Cities that sustain a competitive position are ones that effectively leverage what they have and build up their competitive assets over time, rather than seeking to compete in a sector niche where they have little to offer.

■ **Between neighboring cities with some functional overlap** Within the same country there is some competition for activities that could locate in a choice of cities. Such competition is acutely observed, for example, between Melbourne and Sydney in Australia, between Rio de Janeiro and São Paulo in Brazil, between Barcelona and Madrid in Spain, and between Johannesburg and Cape Town in South Africa. On a continental scale a version of neighbor-to-neighbor competition can be observed between Hong Kong and Singapore in Asia, between London and Paris in Europe, or between Buenos Aires and São Paulo in Latin America.

This does not mean that these neighboring cities compete solely with one another. Indeed, much of their activity is complementary and distinctive. But it does mean that rivalry between neighbors can become intense and even so compelling and absorbing at the local level that other opportunities are underestimated or missed. For many such cities the key requirement is to look beyond the narrow local competition and focus on larger opportunities and markets.

Becoming a global city in the twenty-first century is about learning to compete. It is about productivity. But productivity must be combined with coordination and promotion so that it is well organized and well communicated, and if it is to produce returns over time that justify costs, it should be sustainable. Global cities have to foster a competitive inclination among leaders that understands and welcomes contest, sees it as a spur to innovation and improvement, and embraces benchmarking and comparison. This competitive mental orientation has far-reaching implications for how strategies are developed and resources are deployed, and who contributes to leadership. As cities become more competitive, they utilize insights from business and markets much more in the development of strategy and the process of prioritization.

## TACKLING DEVELOPMENT AND ADJUSTMENT CHALLENGES

The second broad challenge of the future concerns managing growth and success. Globalizing cities can add an additional "transnational" cylinder to their "national" growth engine. The effect can often be rapid increases in population migration, the expansion of international investment, and an increased demand for land, housing, transport, infrastructure, energy, utilities, and public services. The pace and scale of such development and growth may often overwhelm preexisting systems of investment and delivery, leading to deficits, shortages, and acute problems of affordability, livability, pollution, congestion, and inequality.

These challenges in turn may lead to concerns about even longer-term problems that are difficult to resolve within any single cycle of development:

- inequality and political resistance to the global city model,
- loss of productivity and competitiveness, and
- questionable sustainability of the global city model in terms of pollution, overcrowding, and livability.

These issues require governance responses to arrest and address the key growth challenges before they become persistent and long-term issues that are much harder to resolve. In large part this is why investment, governance, coordination, and services provision in globalizing cities have become important arenas of action.

Having discovered how to become competitive and to go global, cities then need to learn how to manage these unintended consequences of success.

For these reasons, metropolitan area governance and investment in globalizing cities are now a major focus of analysis and reform efforts. The basic problem is that very few cities or metro areas are equipped to address these challenges because of combined weaknesses in local and subnational governance. These deficits can be observed in the following areas:

- *Fragmented governance,* the result of neighboring local governments operating with limited coordination and with weak alignment with national and subnational bodies, all with different political leadership cycles and reporting mechanisms.
- *Very limited autonomy,* such that governing power often remains concentrated in upper-level authorities.

- *Fiscal, financial, and investment deficits*, which make planning for infrastructure difficult and force cities to petition to win backing for big projects.
- *Short-termism in political mandates,* which prevents concerted action on the big development challenges, the ones that need twenty to thirty years of continuous action.
- *Scarce national support for global city agendas* owing to siloed sectoral ministries, rural or regional electoral priorities, and regulatory frameworks that unintentionally incentivize negative outcomes.

In this common context, reforming city governance in globalizing cities and developing stronger informal and negotiated governance systems become important endeavours.

### DEVELOPING RELATIONSHIPS WITH NATIONS AND WIDER REGIONS

The third key challenge that globalizing cities face concerns the relationship with their nation-state or the broader state or provincial government. The complex equation of the advantages and disadvantages that globalizing cities bring to national, state, or provincial economies and governments is rarely fully articulated.

On the one hand, globalizing cities can drive national growth through external trade and investment, and can make their nation more productive and specialized.[6] Among the positive externalities global cities are known to provide for their national economies are the following:

- Spending by the international functions that they host increases demand for national goods and services.
- They are transport gateways to the rest of the country for tourists and visitors.
- They are often "escalator regions" that raise the skills of national workers, who later in their career return with increased proficiency.[7]
- They can improve the business brands of nations because they are identified as leading business cities.
- Economic density and business proximity encourage the formation of infrastructure, services, and information that can be shared around the country.
- The tax yield from higher-value industries (such as finance or ICT) can be redistributed to lagging national regions.
- International firms help transfer knowledge to domestic firms and provide access to international markets and international capital.
- Expertise in financing and managing exports can facilitate mass employment in manufacturing industries.

On the other hand, these globalizing cities and their growth drivers can also generate problems for wider regions and nations:

- They can drain other regions of more highly skilled talent, intensifying the territorial disparities in skills within a nation.
- An excessive concentration of higher-value sectors can detract from the growth potential elsewhere.

- National government part-financing of projects happens more regularly than in other, less bankable parts of the country.
- Government monetary and regulatory policy becomes perceived as too oriented toward the needs of global cities and their specialist sectors. Macro policies may be seen to support financial services or digital media rather than manufacturing or logistics, for example.
- Fiscal redistribution may not be viewed as enough to tackle the ever-growing welfare needs in other regions. The risk of entering a near permanent situation in which the same productive regions fiscally support the less productive regions may be seen as suboptimal.

The extent to which these negative externalities are perceived, real, or more significant than the advantages that the global cities bring is hotly debated in many countries. But it is clear that in the future, globalizing cities will need to recruit the support of higher tiers of government to their long-term strategies. Their ability to do so depends on achieving some resolution to this conundrum of how to articulate the value to larger economies and state or national governments and how to align wider systems of governance and economic strategy with the opportunities that global cities bring to other cities and towns within the same domestic economy.

These three overarching challenges for the global city model demand better tools and stronger coalitions for the future.

**LEADERSHIP AND GLOBAL CITIES**    The theme of leadership therefore emerges as critical. Leadership is the means by which global cities can fill gaps in their powers, influence other stakeholders, and align resources and efforts across many different actors. How global cities and their leaders plan for the future, anticipate disruptors, and implement timely changes will likely be key to their ability to remain competitive and globally relevant.

The sphere of city leadership in global cities is drawing on new city networks, business leadership groups, universities, and civic bodies. The institutional and leadership landscape of most global cities will likely become even more dispersed in the future (figure 7-1). This diversity may well boost global cities' resources, ideas, and powers and foster innovation. But a key task for future city leaders will be making this distributed system of leadership more coherent through adopting common strategies, increasing coordination, building partnerships and coalitions, and enacting broader reforms. The following pages review the ways in which global cities are reforming their institutions and expanding their leadership networks to meet the challenge of competing and coping with the externalities of their global success.

**NEW GOVERNANCE FOR GLOBAL CITIES**    Nearly all global cities have grown beyond their historical political and electoral boundaries. For only a minority (such as Istanbul or Shanghai) is most or all of the metro population governed within a single administrative territory. More commonly

FIGURE 7-1.  **THE LEADERSHIP NEXUS FOR GLOBAL CITIES**

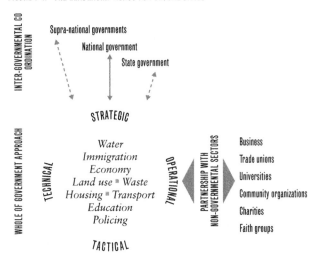

the original core city is dwarfed by the larger metro area. Because most patterns of metropolitan governance are, in effect, accidental outcomes of many cycles of development, there is usually a strong case for reform to give the system the capacity to address questions at the metro scale. This desired scale is impossible to define permanently because the technologies that shape the spatial footprints and travel-to-work patterns—trains, land use patterns, logistics—are constantly in flux.

Increasingly, even metropolitan areas are no longer self-contained but now overlap with other regions. A flexible geometry is therefore essential.

The reform of metropolitan governance systems to catch up with functional reality is happening at very

TABLE 7-1. **TYPES OF GOVERNANCE REFORM IN GLOBAL CITIES SINCE 1990**

| | | |
|---|---|---|
| Rearrangements to government authority | Creation of metro entity that represents municipalities | Barcelona |
| | Supra-municipal elected government and parliament | Stuttgart |
| | Metro authority and directly elected mayor | Seoul |
| | Metro combined authority | Greater Manchester |
| | Shift from two tier to single tier | Johannesburg |
| Boundary changes | Expansion of the boundaries of the metro municipality | Istanbul |
| | New city to absorb expansion | Mumbai |
| Metro partnership agreements | Regional alliance for international promotion | Stockholm |
| | A voluntary metro planning body for economic development | Seattle |
| Reforms of local government | Reduction in the number of municipalities | Berlin |
| | Amalgamation of municipalities | Toronto |

different speeds around the world. Metro governance reforms are assuming a wide variety of formats (table 7-1). Some metropolitan areas are building alliances or powers incrementally (for example, Amsterdam and London). Others are subject to one-off mergers (as took place in Auckland and Toronto) or land extensions (as happened in Moscow).

Debates rage as to whether or not the size and capacity of new metro governance really allow these global cities to become more productive and to manage growth issues.[8] Reforms are often compromised by resident opposition to joining larger conurbations, or are derailed by legal disputes around tax, spending, and policy powers. As a result, not all metro consolidations in global cities manage to achieve greater public sector efficiency or even economic growth.[9] Yet although reforms are rarely perfect and usually involve trade-offs, global cities have illustrated the advantages of adapting their governance. These advantages include the following:

- A more visible *global city leadership* to galvanize local governments, negotiate with higher tiers of government, and promote the city in international markets.
- More strategic approaches to *land-use and economic development* through better infrastructure coordination and more tactical use of public land (box 7-2).
- *Improved coordination*, communication, and trust between previously conflictual municipalities.
- *A stronger investment system*, through aggregated fiscal tools, more attraction to private investors, and

BOX 7-2. SANTIAGO DE CHILE

Santiago de Chile is an example of a hybrid emerging/new global city that is discovering the importance of bestowing more powers on metro government to coordinate land use, housing, and transport infrastructure.

The city's strong growth in recent years, driven first by a commodity boom and later by diversified business and logistics ac-

SANTIAGO DE CHILE

tivities, has occurred within a highly centralized political framework established during the dictatorship of General Pinochet (d. 2006). The return to democracy saw projects in the Metropolitan Region of Santiago left to siloed government departments, which struggled to cooperate with each other. The result was a metropolitan area that for a long time had no visionary leadership to coordinate its assets. Santiago grew to 7 million people across six provinces and with more than fifty local governments, but suffered from sprawl, fragmented transport, inequality, and a lack of adequate housing to support its globalizing roles as a regional business headquarters.

A new cycle of reform has begun to address Santiago's deficit. In 2015 and 2016, bills were passed through parliament allowing regional governors to be elected, while granting them more authority over local economic and spatial planning and more financial autonomy. The full extent of the reforms is still to be confirmed, but economic development and infrastructure powers, as well as regional service provision, are on course to be integrated with newly elected regional governors. This marks a dramatic shift in Santiago's ability to steer its economic and spatial development and ultimately shape its own fortunes.

more confidence shown by higher tiers of government for devolution or project cost sharing.

- *Bolder practices* around city branding and innovation systems, and a more future-oriented public discourse.

As global cities look ahead to the future, there is no one right model to follow. Instead they rely on an institutional framework that allows room for a high degree of negotiated collaboration, and on regular dialogue about future goals and priorities. Global cities will need recognition and new laws from the governments above them, but critically, they need buy-in for change from those outside government—citizens, civil society, and business.

## The Role of Civil Society

Most global cities inherit their way of engaging citizens and extragovernmental organizations based on tradition and the political culture. The ability of civic organizations to engage in the process of developing their global cities depends on the depth of social networks and the internal capacity of governments. That said, civic organizations are increasing their roles in global cities as the imperative grows to make sure that governance is democratic and responsive.

Today global cities are experimenting with a number of new ways to engage citizens:

- smart city and future city platforms that engage citizens directly,
- participatory democracy and budget setting,
- social networks and digital communities,
- local NGOs taking the lead in area management and services, and
- crowdfunding and impact bonds.

Positive examples of civic engagement have been seen in Rio de Janeiro, Toronto, Johannesburg, and Cape Town, and in many cases civic bodies have become a genuine source of innovation and inclusion (box 7-3).[10]

## The Role of Business Leadership Organizations

As highlighted in some of the examples in earlier chapters, business leaders have a very long history of engaging in the process of city development, from the early merchants guilds and boards of trade all the way to the chambers of commerce in the eighteenth and nineteenth centuries. Since the 1980s a resurgence of proactive business leadership has become visible all over the world. Often comprising a small number of business leaders of large companies or influential entrepreneurs, so-called business leadership organizations are playing an influential role in decisionmaking in global cities as diverse as Barcelona, Bogota, London, and Sydney. Not all such bodies represent exclusively the private sector, as some invite civic bodies and nongovernmental organizations (NGOs) to take part. What is common to most, however, is a developmental, metropolitan, and comparative perspective that adds a valuable angle on how to promote and achieve competitiveness in a global system (box 7-4).

Because these business leadership groups are often organizationally lean, they are able to provide a source of leadership for global city development without being entangled in institutional obligations. This means they are able to look beyond four- or five-year electoral cycles and the confines of political geography in the interests of the whole metro area. Their members also have valuable experience in activities that have become relevant to global cities, such as branding, sales, and setting agendas. In new global and emerging global cities they help the process of

BOX 7-3. JOHANNESBURG—GAUTENG

The Gauteng City Region is home to 13 million people and produces a third of South Africa's GDP. It is the country's gateway to the world but faces severe inequality, housing, and spatial integration challenges. The Gauteng City-Region Observatory (GCRO) was set up in 2008 by the University of Johannesburg and the University of Witswatersrand, in collaboration with the Gauteng Provincial Government and local authorities. As a metro-wide strategic intelligence provider, it is a unique body that effectively bridges the public and academic divide to support the globalizing city's region's functions through evidence-based analysis.

The GCRO has helped reduce governance fragmentation in a region with several metropolitan and municipal governments, including those of Johannesburg and Tshwane. It collects data, benchmarks the city region, and provides both policy analysis and independent research on its needs and challenges. Many of its tools in data analytics and infographics are world class, including quality-of-life surveys, longitudinal policy barometers, and international comparisons. As such, the GCRO offers an integrated view of local problems, opportunities, and solutions to local leaders, businesses, and civil society and gives these individuals and entities the knowledge and focus necessary to cooperate. It fills a capacity cap that the public sector did not have the means to tackle, and it brings academics and policymakers into closer contact in a way that few global regions have achieved. By harmonizing data and boosting knowledge exchange, the GCRO has helped planners and citizens make sense of what might otherwise be a highly fragmented region.

BOX 7-4.  BUSINESS LEADERSHIP: SYDNEY AND BARCELONA

Business leadership groups play a variety of roles in global cities, depending on the existing governance shortfalls in the city. In some cities they have even come to play a direct strategic and thought leadership role in tandem with government.

SYDNEY. The Committee for Sydney makes an important intellectual contribution by advocating for a properly managed Sydney metro area. Its membership includes major businesses, universities, NGOs, and local governments, all focusing on the future of Sydney's planning and governance, transport, quality of life, and competitiveness. Its findings inform decisionmaking by New South Wales state departments, and it has partnered with the NSW Department of Trade and Investment to launch a Global Talent Hub Project, in search of new ways to turn local skills into global assets.

The Committee for Sydney also plays a role in highlighting Sydney's pivot to innovation and technology, showcasing the value of "density done well" and outlining an integrated vision for Sydney's future up to 2055. The Committee therefore fills a gap in Sydney's governance, offering a globally informed and evidence-led take on the long-term challenges for Sydney, where public policy has been slow to emerge.

BARCELONA. For a different kind of business leadership group, in cities where metro governance may be more established but the economic strategy is less clear, the organizing principle has been to make the city more attractive to talent and high-value economic sectors. Barcelona Global is one such organization.

Continued

Privately run, fully funded by its members, and open to the city's most influential business leaders, companies, and professionals, it explicitly seeks to make Barcelona one of Europe's top ten global cities, thanks to a concentration of talent, investment, internationalized sectors, and the power of the Barcelona brand.

Barcelona Global has taken the initiative, often in partnership with public authorities, to boost Barcelona's skills base and English-language uptake and to reduce red tape. It also offers vital market intelligence, running a perception survey of Barcelona's strengths and weaknesses abroad, creating a fiscal benchmark to assess its global tax position, and overseeing a regular survey called the Talent Monitor, which asks the city's international residents and investors what works and what could be improved in the city. Other achievements include bringing Startup Bootcamp to Barcelona, promoting entrepreneurship in local schools, and developing tools to track the city's position on digital media. Barcelona Global also lobbies strongly for greater metro coordination and is seen as a key source of vision and leadership in the promotion of Barcelona as a global city.

internationalization by bringing to bear international experience through their networks in other countries, and can reveal unfamiliar demand-side opportunities. There are many examples of business leadership groups helping to raise awareness in global cities about the case for immigration, solutions to the housing supply, and the social dividend of greater infrastructure capacity.[11] There is little doubt that business leadership is here to stay in global cities, as evidenced by the new networks and initiatives such as World Economic Forum's Global Agenda Council for Infrastructure and Urban Development, the World Business Council for Sustainable Development, and the Global Cities Business Alliance.

COMMON FUTURE AGENDAS   The opportunities and the risks for global cities, whether those cities are established, emerging, or new on the scene, mean that a new attitude toward the future is taking shape (box 7-5). Cities are engaged in scenario-building exercises and horizon scanning to map the full implications of future change, and then to inform and prepare citizens, governments, and investors of the imperatives for future development. These scans of the future highlight at least four areas of strategic importance for global cities going forward: agility in the face of economic change, ability to manage the consequences of growth, a system of governance that is fit for purpose, and the financial wherewithal to deliver change.

*Agility amid global economic change.* In each cycle of globalization, different sectors globalize at differential speeds, and cities find they have competitive advantage in regional and global markets. The cycle beginning in 2008–09 has seen the globalization of higher education, clean technology, and life sciences, but the sectors that globalize in the next two or three cycles will be different. More than 100 cities are also competing for industrial production within very fast-moving value chains where the cost-benefit calculus is constantly shifting. This degree of competition highlights that it is now rare for cities to grow in multiple economic cycles without changing tack with each cycle. This means that any cities seeking to

BOX 7-5. THE FUTURE OF CITIES: LONDON, SÃO PAULO, AND SAN DIEGO

Cities with different assets and opportunities are preparing for the future in different ways.

LONDON. For an *established global city* such as London, twenty-five years of success means that today its population is heading toward 10 million people, and the city has to be proactive in mobilizing resources accordingly. A London Infrastructure Plan up to 2050 has been adopted by a new Infrastructure Delivery Board, which makes clear what system needs will have to met. The plan gives confidence to public and private actors that London has a clear idea of what it needs and how that can be achieved, and this has translated into support for the next big rail project, Crossrail 2. London is also moving to address liveability and land supply. The Smart London Plan develops potential synergies between its tech economy, infrastructure networks, and civil society to help improve the performance of key systems. Land supply has been the focus of a new Land Commission, which identifies public sector brownfield land and has already found enough space for 130,000 homes in the coming development cycle. London is also building consensus for greater fiscal tools and autonomy to address future challenges.

SÃO PAULO. For an *emerging global city* such as São Paulo, which is now Latin America's major centre for business capitalization, real estate, and innovation, the future challenge is twofold. First, the city must build metropolitan systems (housing, rail, water, sanitation, flood defense) that are fit for purpose. Second, it must increase the rate of investment in urban quality in order to transition into services and higher-value sectors. A faster pace of transport development requires funding, delivery capacity, and environmental licensing. In the future, the city will have to partner with higher tiers of government to overhaul regulations that thwart reinvestment. Despite some successes with *urban operations* to transform slums into high-quality social housing through the sale of additional development rights, the city should develop more effective public-private partnerships to engage the private sector more broadly in inclusive redevelopment. For São Paulo, recent overdue reforms to recognize metropolitan areas and re-negotiate the city's interest rates are welcome, but the city will only be able to implement transformative change through fiscal reform and better incentives for government alignment and cooperation. São Paulo's business leadership will likely also have to play a bigger role to build a common reform agenda around transparency, safety, and business climate.

SAN DIEGO. For *new global cities* with a shorter history of global engagement, the future demands more intense collaboration to increase exports and trade links. San Diego has recognized the need to fully leverage its skills base, thriving innovation economy, access to Mexico and the Pacific, major anchors, and quality of life. For the last few years the city leadership has been building cross-sector regional collaboration to connect local firms to global markets, secure foreign direct investment, and upgrade the region's airport and port infrastructure. A competition, Metro-Connect, offers funding to export-ready small and medium-sized enterprises to enable them to access the resources to internationalize. Another project, the Export Roadmap, helps simplify the process of exporting for local actors. Attempts to enhance San Diego's brand are under way and Discover San Diego events held to attract international attention. The combined organized expertise of university and business leaders allows smaller global cities such as San Diego to achieve global relevance and leadership.

create a framework for growth, competitiveness, and inclusion must develop fine-grained approaches to building their skills base, managing their business climate, and supplying the requisite real estate for the future economy. For every city, this will entail devising a mix of long-term strategy, medium-term tactics, and short-term catalysts. The craft of long-term economic development is one that only some cities will get right, but the returns will be substantial.

**Adaptation to the consequences of growth.** When cities globalize over one or two cycles, it is common for them to rub up against a series of constraints or externalities. These include price inflation (for goods and housing), an undersupply of housing relative to demand, entrenched opposition between asset owners and asset renters, deficits in public transport infrastructure, and the emergence of a "two-speed" economy in which middle-income jobs shrink and hostility to globalization grows. Many of these problems are unanticipated by city governments during the initial cycles of growth and can later come to appear almost intractable. The future prosperity of global cities will partly depend on how quickly they learn how to keep growing in a managed and coherent way, not least by unlocking development through new infrastructure.

**Governance fit for a global city.** There is a growing consensus that global cities will be unable to address the externalities of their success unless they develop better systems of governance. To do so means overcoming inherited political geographies and collaborating across functional economic geographies so that the city can grow and compete as one unit. Global cities are finding different ways forward in this area, whether through big one-off reforms, incremental adjustments, or more collaborative leadership coalitions. The governance challenge also means overcoming siloed approaches to issues that should be addressed in an integrated way, and this often needs the support of higher tiers of government.

**Capital to deliver change.** It has rapidly become apparent that most global cities are underinvested relative to their growth and maintenance needs. This situation has arisen even though there is a vast pool of global capital (belonging to international development banks, sovereign wealth funds, pension funds, private equity houses, or other private investors) searching for investment projects. The reasons for underinvestment often have to do with centralized fiscal systems that leave cities dependent on upper levels of government for grants and transfers. Many cities also have surprisingly limited tools to borrow capital, raise revenue locally, or capture the value of development over the full life cycle of infrastructure. Moreover, knowledge about how to optimize and package city assets to attract external investment is often profoundly lacking. Again, global cities are adopting different solutions to these deficits, and their ability to partner and negotiate with government and with private sector entities is key.

**FUTURE DILEMMAS AND POINTS OF DEPARTURE**   Nearly all cities face these four strategic questions in their own way, but from very different starting points and in very different institutional conditions. In this rich context, many distinct issues arise for certain global cities and systems of cities as they think about securing their futures.

For global cities where national governments have become very remote or even detached from their concerns the key question is whether a partnership for success with the nation state can be reestablished or whether the city has to go it alone and devise its own global path for the rest of this century. Cities such as Cape Town, Mumbai, and New York face versions of this dilemma, as their national governments fail to deliver reforms or investments that are essential to their productive and inclusive growth.

For global cities in more centralized systems a different question arises: how to win support from national government for key projects and devolutionary powers, while at the same time ensuring that other cities can also thrive and that national political support for its global roles is not withdrawn. London, Seoul, Tokyo, and Warsaw all face different versions of this dilemma. Meanwhile, other global cities face the mixed blessing of a highly interventionist national government whose decisionmaking may be short-sighted or erratic. Learning how to engage tactically and successfully with national governments will become a key yardstick for global cities in the future.[12]

Another question that is now on the radar for global cities is the extent to which partnerships between business and governing institutions will become necessary or desirable. Globalized cities and globalized businesses are becoming increasingly interdependent. The interconnections are evident in the reurbanization of business in city centers, the emergence of cities as target business markets, the urbanization of capital and of innovation, and the rise of city building itself as an international business sector in its own right.

As a result of these relationships, businesses are increasingly helping global cities tackle their development challenges. This happens not only through the adoption by cities of private sector practices and organizational tools. It also means business taking a lead in city partnerships, such as Cisco in Bangalore and Manchester or Arup with the C40 Cities Climate Leadership Group. How global cities manage the benefits and pitfalls of these arrangements and learn to optimize the engagement of the private sector will be an important area of differentiation in the future.

Population change, sustainability, geopolitics, economic specialization, managed growth, metro governance, nation-state partnerships, and business leadership—all add up to one inescapable message. There will be more ways than ever for cities to become global cities, more types of global cities than ever, and more differences between them as they try to manage the multi-headed hydra of being a global city.

SUMMARY     As the next cycles of globalization play out, the pattern of global cities on each continent will take shape in different ways. The scenario that transpires on each continent will, however, eventually look quite similar: a mix of mature global cities and newer globalizing cities, playing different and distinctive roles.

In Europe, for example, four cities are expected to have the size, scale, and diversity to host a full range of global functions—Istanbul, London, Moscow, and Paris. These will be supported by a powerful cadre of ten to fifteen high-quality second cities, including Amsterdam, Barcelona, Manchester, Munich, Oslo, Stockholm, and Vienna, that will play outsized roles in the global innovation and visitor economies.

Meanwhile, in Asia, current trends suggest that a group of six established world cities will be settled by 2030—Hong Kong, Seoul, Singapore, and Tokyo, joined by Beijing and Shanghai. Each of these cities will likely be complemented by other global cities in their regional cluster, specializing in technology, trade, and advanced manufacturing (such as Shenzhen, Tianjin, Nanjing, and Osaka). Many other cities are also creating important niches for international institutions (Manila), visitor attractions (Colombo, Xi'an), or software (Bangalore, Ho Chi Minh City).

For each and every one of these cities, the appropriate calculus connecting population, tradable industries, connectivity, quality, and resilience will have to be determined according to their own unique stories and solutions.

Similar systems of global cities might in the future be observed in North America, Latin America, and Africa. This is the history we now inhabit. It is a distinctive period in the life of the human race, when, as populations urbanize over the next seventy-five years until a stable population level is reached and systems of cities have settled and matured, not one or two global cities will be found on each continent but thirty or forty.

These continental systems of cities will continue to adapt and evolve. But the fundamental shape and pattern will be determined in the coming five decades as trade relationships and infrastructure investments, supported by social, cultural, and political collaboration, foster new leagues and routes that have their antecedents in the past but are embedded in the future.

These new patterns may well seem familiar, even if they are intensely modern. They reflect the short history of the global cities, as we know them, and they magnify the story of their cities as a means to observe our modern world.

# SOURCES FOR BOXES AND FIGURES

*The Hanseatic League (Box 2-1)*
Mark Kurlansky, *Salt: A World History* (London: Vintage, 2003).
Henri Pirenne, *Medieval Cities: Their Origins and the Revival of Trade* (Princeton University Press, 2014 [1969]).
Raf Verbruggen, Michael Hoyler, and Peter Taylor, "The Networked City," in *Atlas of Cities,* edited by Paul Know (Princeton University Press, 2014), pp. 34–51.

*The Original Global Cities: Athens, Alexandria, Rome (Box 3-1)*
Robin Osborne and Andrew Wallace-Hadrill, "Cities of the Ancient Mediterranean," in *The Oxford Handbook of Cities in World History*, edited by Peter Clark (Oxford University Press, 2013), pp. 49–65.
Brigitte Truschnegg, "Phenomenon of Global Cities in the Ancient World," in *Globalization and the City: Two Connected Phenomena in Past and Present*, edited by Andreas Exenberger and others (Innsbruck University Press, 2013), pp. 75–102.
Lila Leontidou and Guido Martinotti, "The Foundational City," in *Atlas of Cities,* edited by Paul Know (Princeton University Press, 2014), pp. 16–33.

*Global Cities of the Chinese Dynasties (Box 3-2)*
John King Fairbank and Merle Goldman, *China: A New History* (Belknap Press of Harvard University Press, 2006).
Peter Rimmer and Howard Dick, "The Historical Dimension," in *Global City Challenges: Debating a Concept, Improving the Practice,* edited by Michele Acuto and Wendy Steele (Basingstoke: Palgrave Macmillan, 2013), pp. 63–87.
George William Skinner, "Introduction: Urban Development in Imperial China," in *The City in Late Imperial China*, edited by George William Skinner (Stanford University Press, 1977), pp. 3–32.
On Hangzhou: Janet Abu Lughod, *Before European Hegemony* (Oxford University Press, 1989).

*Capital of World Trade: Tenth-Century Baghdad (Box 3-3)*
Peter Frankopan, *The Silk Roads: A New History of the World* (London: Bloomsbury, 2015).

*London: Evolution of International Stock Exchanges, Insurance, and Banking (Box 3-4)*
British Banking History Society, "The Birth of the English Cheque," 2009 (www.infobritain.co.uk/).
Ann M. Carlos and Larry Neal, "Amsterdam and London as Financial Centers in the Eighteenth Century," *Financial History Review* 18, no.1 (2011), pp. 21–46.
Markman Ellis, *The Coffee House: A Cultural History* (London: Orion Publishing Group, 2004), p. 167.
John Biddulph Martin, *The Grasshopper in Lombard Street* (New York: Scribner and Welford, 1892), p. 207.
Illustration: Thomas Rowlandson and Augustus Charles Pugin. In William Henry Pyne and William Combe, *The Microcosm of London or London in Miniature,* vol.3 (London: Methuen and Company).

*Guangzhou: Compelled Global City (Box 4-1)*
Roy Moxham, *Tea: Addiction, Exploitation and Empire* (London: Robinson, 2003).
Luc-Normand Tellier, *Urban World History: An Economic and Geographical Perspective* (Presses de l'Université de Quebec, 2009), pp. 331–96.

Steven Wallech and others, *World History: A Concise Thematic Analysis*, vol. 2 (Oxford: Wiley-Blackwell, 2013).


*Los Angeles: Global City of Entertainment (Box 4-2)*
Edward W. Soja and Allen J. Scott, "Introduction to Los Angeles: City and Region," in *The City: Los Angeles and Urban Theory at the End of the Twentieth Century,* edited by Allen J. Scott and Edward W. Soja (University of California Press, 1996), pp. 1–21.
Luc-Normand Tellier, *Urban World History: An Economic and Geographical Perspective* (Presses de l'Université de Quebec, 2009), pp. 331–96.
Brookings, *The Ten Traits of Globally Fluent Metro Areas: Los Angeles* (2013).


*Tokyo: From Megacity to Global City (Box 4-3)*
Kuniko Fujita, "Neo-Industrial Tokyo: Urban Development and Globalization in Japan's State-Centred Developmental Capitalism," *Urban Studies* 40, no. 2 (2003), pp. 249–81.
Asato Saito and Andy Thornley, "Shifts in Tokyo's World City Status and the Urban Planning Response," *Urban Studies* 40, no. 4 (2003), pp. 665–85.
Andre Sorensen, "Building World City Tokyo: Globalization and Conflict over Urban Space," *Annals of Regional Science* 37, no. 3 (2003), pp. 519–31.
Eleanor Westney, "Changing Perspectives on the Organization of Japanese Multinational Companies," in *Japanese Multinationals Abroad*, edited by Schon L. Beecher and Allan Bird (Oxford University Press, 1999), pp. 11–30.


*San Francisco: City of Discovery and Innovation (Box 4-4)*
Michael Storper and others, *The Rise and Fall of Urban Economies* (Stanford University Press, 2015).
Photo: Gerald P. Hawkins


*Globalization and World Cities (GaWC) (Box 5-1)*
Ben Derudder and others, "Pathways of Growth and Decline: Connectivity Changes in the World City Network, 2000–2008," *Urban Studies* 47, no. 9 (2010), pp. 1861–77.

*Definitions of and Statements about Global Cities over Time (Box 5-2)*

Jonathan. V. Beaverstock, Richard. G. Smith, and Peter J. Taylor, "A Roster of World Cities," *Cities* 16, no. 6 (1999), pp. 445–58.

Derek Gregory, Ron Johnston, Geraldine Pratt, Michael Watts, Sarah Whatmore, *The Dictionary of Human Geography* (Oxford: Blackwell, 2009), p. 811.

Newman Grubb and Knight Frank, *Global Cities: The 2016 Report* (2016) (www.knightfrank.com/resources/global-cities /2016/all/global-cities-the-2016-report.pdf).

Ann Markus and Vicky Gwiasda (1994), quoted in David Gladstone and Susan Fainstein, "The New York and Los Angeles Economics," in *New York and Los Angeles: Politics, Society, and Culture. A Comparative View,* edited by David Halle (University of Chicago Press, 2003), p. 85.

Saskia Sassen, "The Global City: Introducing a Concept," *Brown Journal of World Affairs* 11, no. 2 (2005), p. 40.

John Rennie Short, *Global Metropolitan: Globalizing Cities in a Capitalist World* (New York: Routledge, 2004), p. 2.

James Tyner, "Labouring in the Periphery: The Place of Manila in the Global Economy," in *Relocating Global Cities: From the Center to the Margins,* edited by Michael Amen, Kevin Archer, and M. Martin Bosman (Lanham, Md.: Rowman and Littlefield, 2006), p. 114.


*New York: Where the World Does Business (Box 6-1)*

Brookings, "The Ten Traits of Globally Fluent Metro Areas: New York,"2013 (www.brookings.edu/~/media/Multimedia /Interactives/2013/tentraits/New York.pdf).

Brookings, "Export Monitor 2015," 2015 (www.brookings.edu /research/interactives/2015/export-monitor#10420).

Greg Clark and Tim Moonen, *Technology, Real Estate and the Innovation Economy* (London: Urban Land Institute, 2015) (http://europe.uli.org/wp-content/uploads/sites/3/ULI-Documents /FINAL-Innovation-Report1.pdf).

Saskia Sassen, *Cities in a World Economy* (London: Sage, 2012).

Luc-Normad Tellier, *Urban World History: An Economic and Geographical Perspective* (Presses de l'Université de Quebec, 2009), pp. 331–96.

*Istanbul: Back to the Future with Europe's Newest Global City*
*(Box 6-2)*

Euromonitor, *Top 100 City Destinations Ranking*, 2016 (http://
blog.euromonitor.com/2016/01/top-100-city-destinations
-ranking-2016.html).

A. Faruk Goksu and Sila Akapl, *Restructuring of Istanbul: Re-
connection, Regeneration, Resettlement* (GYODER and Istanbul Chamber of Commerce, 2015) (www.gyoder.org.tr/img/mc
-content/201503181718582622restructuring-of-istanbul—mipim
-2015.pdf).

JLL, *Istanbul on the World Stage*, 2016 (www.jll.com.tr/turkey
/en-gb/research/istanbul-on-the-world-stage).

OECD, *OECD Territorial Reviews: Istanbul, Turkey* (Paris: OECD,
2008).

Deyan Sudjic, "The City Too Big To Fail," in Ricky Burdett, ed.,
*Istanbul: City of Intersections* (London: Urban Age, 2009),
pp. 3–4.

Z/Yen and Long Finance, *The Global Financial Centres Index 19*,
2016 (www.longfinance.net/publications.html?id=953).


*Strategic Imperatives for Many Established Global Cities*
*(Box 6-3)*

Adapted from Greg Clark, Tim Moonen, and Jonathan Couturier, *Globalisation and Competition: The New World of Cities*
(London: JLL, 2015) (www.jll.com/research/158/jll-globalization
-and-competition-the-new-world-of-cities).


*Strategic Imperatives for Many Emerging Global Cities*
*(Box 6-4)*

Adapted from Greg Clark, Tim Moonen, and Jonathan Couturier, *Globalisation and Competition: The New World of Cities*
(London: JLL, 2015) (www.jll.com/research/158/jll-globaliza
tion-and-competition-the-new-world-of-cities).


*Strategic Imperatives for New Global Cities (Box 6-5)*
Greg Clark, Tim Moonen, and Jonathan Couturier, *Globalisation and Competition: The New World of Cities.*

*The New Silk Road: One Belt, One Road (Box 7-1)*

Tim Winter, "One Belt, One Road, One Heritage: Cultural Diplomacy and the Silk Road," *The Diplomat* (March2016) (http://
thediplomat.com/2016/03/one-belt-one-road-one-heritage
-cultural-diplomacy-and-the-silk-road/).


*Santiago de Chile (Box 7-2)*

Rosario Alvarez, "Más atribuciones, financiamiento y elección de
intendentes: Los proyectos del gobierno para la regionalización,"
Nacional, April 14, 2015 (www.latercera.com/noticia/nacional
/2015/04/680-625435-9-mas-atribuciones-financiamiento-y
-eleccion-de-intendentes-los-proyectos-del.shtml).

Macarena Fernández, "Santiago no es Chile: Luz verde para la
votación popular de intendentes," *El Definido*, January 29,
2016 (www.eldefinido.cl/actualidad/pais/6431/Santiago-no-es
-Chile-luz-verde-para-la-votacion-popular-de-intendentes/).

Geraldie Pflieger, "Santiago de Chile—Prototype of the Neo-
liberal City: Between a Strong State and Privatised Public Services," in *Governing Megacities in Emerging Countries*, edited
by Dominique Lorrain (Farnham: Ashgate, 2014), pp. 217–68.

Jesus Leal Trujillo, Joseph Parilla, and Slaven Razmilic, *Global
Santiago: Profiling the Metropolitan Region's International
Competitiveness and Connections* (Brookings, 2016).

Photo: Jorgebarrios, El Barrio Pedro de Valdivia Norte.


*Johannesburg—Gauteng (Box 7-3)*

Gauteng City Region Observatory, "Vision, Mandate and Core
Roles," 2016 (www.gcro.ac.za/about/about-the-gcro).

Gauteng City Region Observatory, "The Gauteng City Region,"
2016 (www.gcro.ac.za/about/the-gauteng-city-region/).

OECD, *OECD Territorial Reviews: The Gauteng City-Region,
South Africa* (Paris: OECD, 2011) (www.gautengonline.gov.za
/Documents/oecd-territorial-reviews-the-gauteng-city-region
-south-africa-2011_5kg6z886dbmr.pdf).


*Business Leadership: Barcelona and Sydney (Box 7-4)*

Barcelona Global, "About Us," 2016 (www.barcelonaglobal.com
/about-us/barcelona-global).

Barcelona Global, *Barcelona and Its Future* (2014) (www
.barcelonaglobal.com/Resources/public/images/documents
/relacionades/1390734112/en/barcelona-and-its-future-2014
.pdf).

Barcelona Global, "Projects," 2016 (www.barcelonaglobal.com
/projects).

Committee for Sydney, "About Us," 2016 (www.sydney.org.au
/who-we-are/about-us/).

Committee for Sydney, "Projects and Research," 2016 (www
.sydney.org.au/what-we-do/projects/).

Committee for Sydney, "Taskforces," 2016 (www.sydney.org.au
/what-we-do/task-forces/).

Committee for Sydney, "2016–17 Priorities," 2015 (www.sydney
.org.au/wp-content/uploads/2015/10/CfS-Priorities-2016-17-1
.pdf).

KPMG and the Committee for Sydney, *Unlocking the Potential:
the Fintech Opportunity for Sydney* (2014) (www.sydney.org
.au/wp-content/uploads/2015/08/CfS-Unlocking-the-Potential
-the-Fintech-opportunity-for-Sydney-2014.pdf).

*The Future of Cities: London, São Paulo, and San Diego*
*(Box 7-5)*

Greg Clark and Tim Moonen, "International Background Report
for the New York Fourth Regional Plan—Global City Regions:
Case Studies and Good Practice. How Are the World's Leading
Regions Tackling Their Long Term Challenges?" (unpublished,
2015).

Greater London Authority, *Smart London Plan: Using the Creative Power of New Technologies to Serve London and Improve
Londoners' Lives* (2013) (www.london.gov.uk/sites/default/files
/smart_london_plan.pdf).

San Diego Regional Economic Development Corporation and
Brookings, *Go Global: San Diego's Global Trade and Investment Initiative* (Brookings, 2015) (www.sandiegobusiness.org
/sites/default/files/Go%20Global%20-%20San%20Diego's%20
Global%20Trade%20and%20Investment%20Initiative.pdf).

San Diego Business Council, "World Trade Center San Diego,"
2016 (www.sandiegobusiness.org/wtcsd).

# NOTES

*1. Navigating Global Cities*

1. See Globalisation and World Cities Network, "The World According to GaWC 2012," 2013 (www.lboro.ac.uk/gawc /world2012t.html).

*2. Origins: Trade and Connectivity*

1. Philip Curtin, *Cross-Cultural Trade in World History* (Cambridge University Press, 1984).

2. Masahisa Fujita, Paul Krugman and Anthony Venables, *The Spatial Economy: Cities, Regions, and International Trade* (MIT Press, 2001).

3. Luc-Normand Tellier, *Urban World History: An Economic and Geographical Perspective* (Presses de l'Université de Quebec, 2009), pp. 331–96.

4. Volker Bornschier and Peter Lengye, *Waves, Formations and Values in the World System* (New Brunswick, N.J.: Transaction, 1992).

5. Pierre Briant, *From Cyrus to Alexander: A History of the Persian Empire*, translated byPeter T. Daniels (Winona Lake, IN: Eisenbrauns, 2002; first published Paris: Librairie Arthème Fayard, 1996).

6. Michael C. Howard, *Transnationalism in Ancient and Medieval Societies: The Role of Cross-Border Trade and Travel* (Jefferson, N.C.: McFarland and Co., 2012).

7. Christopher I. Beckwith, *Empires of the Silk Road: A History of Central Eurasia from the Bronze Age to the Present* (Princeton University Press, 2009), p. 328

8. Ibid.

9. Peter Frankopan, *The Silk Roads: A New History of the World* (London: Bloomsbury, 2015). See also UNESCO, "Silk Road: Interactive Map of the Cities along the Silk Roads," 2016 (http://en.unesco.org/silkroad/network-silk-road-cities-map-app /en).

10. Oscar Gelderblom, *Cities of Commerce: The Institutional Foundations of International Trade in the Low Countries, 1250–1650* (Princeton University Press, 2013).

11. François Gipouloux, *The Asian Mediterranean: Port Cities and Trading Networks in China, Japan and South East Asia 13th–21st Century* (Cheltenham: Edward Elgar, 2011).

12. Tijl Vanneste, *Global Trade and Commercial Networks: Eighteenth-Century Diamond Merchants* (London: Routledge, 2016).

13. Richard Sennett, *The Fall of Public Man* (Cambridge University Press, 1974).

14. Barry Buzan and George Lawson, *The Global Transformation: History, Modernity and the Making of International Relations* (Cambridge University Press, 2015), pp. 186–87.

15. Gipouloux, *The Asian Mediterranean*.

16. Samuel Fallows, Edmund Buckley, and Shailer Mathews, in *The World To-Day: A Monthly Record of Human Progress* 5 (1903), p. 1446.

17. Philip McCann and Zoltan J. Acs, "Globalization: Countries, Cities and Multinationals," *Regional Studies* 45, no. 1 (2011), pp. 17–32.

18. Richard Baldwin, "Global Supply Chains: Why They Emerged, Why They Matter, and Where They Are Going," in *Global Value Chains in a Changing World*, edited by Deborah K. Elms and Patrick Low (Geneva: World Trade Organization, 2013), pp. 13–60 (www.wto.org/english/res_e/booksp _e/aid4tradeglobalvalue13_e.pdf).

19. Anthony D. King, *Global Cities: Post-Imperialism and the Internationalisation of London* (New York: Routledge Library Editions, 1990).

20. R. C. Feenstra, "Integration of Trade and Disintegration of Production in the Global Economy," *Journal of Economic Perspectives* 12, no. 4 (1998), pp. 31–50.

21. Donald Water, ed., *Global Logistics: New Directions in Supply Chain Management.* (London: KoganPage, 2010).

*3. The History of Global Cities I: Ancient Cities*

1. Martin Pitts and Miguel J. Versluys, "Globalisation and the Roman World: Perspectives and Opportunities," in *Globalisation and the Roman World: Archaeological and Theoretical Perspectives*, edited by Martin Pitts (Cambridge University Press, 2015), pp. 3–31.

2. Frankopan, *The Silk Roads*, p. 12.

3. Yale H. Ferguson and Richard W. Mansnach, *Globalization: The Return of Borders to a Borderless World?* (New York: Routledge, 2012).

4. Polybius, quoted in Pitts and Versluys, "Globalisation and the Roman World," p. 18.

5. Robert Clifford Ostergren and Mathias Le Boss, *The Europeans: A Geography of People, Culture, and Environment* (London: Guildford Press, 2011).

6. Quoted in Karl Moore and David Charles Lewis, *The Origins of Globalization* (New York: Routledge, 2009), p. 57.

7. Tellier, *Urban World History*, pp. 75–93.

8. Janet Abu-Lughod, *Before European Hegemony: The World System A.D. 1250–1350* (Oxford University Press, 1989).

9. Jonathan Bloom and Sheila Blair, *Islam: A Thousand Years of Power and Faith* (Yale University Press, 2002); Fatema Soudavar Farmanfarmainan, "Politics and Patronage: The Evolution of the Sara-ye Amir in the Bazar of Tehran," in *The Bazaar in the Islamic City: Design, Culture, and History,* edited by Mohammad Gharipour (American University in Cairo Press, 2012), p. 206.

10. Pitts and Versluys, "Globalisation and the Roman World," pp. 3–31.

11. Kenneth Pomeranz, *The Great Divergence: China, Europe, and the Making of the Modern World Economy* (Princeton

University Press, 2000) (https://books.google.co.uk/books?id=hSxACQAAQBAJ).

12. Jorge Canizares-Esguerra and others, *The Black Urban Atlantic in the Age of the Slave Trade* (University of Pennsylvania Press, 2013).

13. Aparna Banerjee, "Trade and Urbanisation in pre-independent India: A Historical Perspective," *Journal of History and Social Sciences* 3, no.1 (January–June 2012); Sanjeev Sanyal, *Land of Seven Rivers: History of India's Geography* (London: Penguin, 2012).

14. Oscar Gelderblom, *Cities of Commerce: The Institutional Foundations of International Trade in the Low Countries, 1250–1650* (Princeton University Press, 2013); Mary Lindemann, *The Merchant Republics: Amsterdam, Antwerp, and Hamburg, 1648–1790* (Cambridge University Press, 2015); Tellier, *Urban World History*, pp. 75–93; Alex Woolf, *A Short History of the World* (London: Arcturus Publishing, 2012).

15. Kirsten Mann, *Slavery and the Birth of an African City: Lagos 1760–1900* (Indiana University Press, 2007).

16. Peter N. Stearns, *Globalization in World History* (New York: Routledge, 2010).

17. Alison Rowland, "The Conditions of Life for the Masses," in *Early Modern Europe: An Oxford History*, edited by Euan Cameron (Oxford University Press, 2001), pp. 31–62.

18. Frankopan, *The Silk Roads*.

## 4. The History of Global Cities II: Modern Cities

1. Feisal Farah, "The Metamorphosis of Slavery in Colonial Mombasa, 1907–1963," in *Slavery in Africa and the Caribbean*, edited by Olatunji Ojo and Nadine Hunt (London: IB Tauris, 2012)

2. Tellier, *Urban World History*.

3. Tristram Hunt, *Ten Cities That Made an Empire* (London: Penguin, 2014).

4. Steven Beller, *Vienna and the Jews, 1867–1938: A Cultural History* (Cambridge University Press, 1989); European Foundation for the Improvement of Living and Working Conditions, *Housing and Segregation of Migrants—Case Study: Vienna, Austria* (2009) (www.eurofound.europa.eu/sites/default

/files/ef_files/pubdocs/2009/496/en/1/EF09496EN.pdf); Robert Musil, "The Evolution of a Global City: Vienna's Integration into the World City System," in *Globalization and the City: Two Connected Phenomena in Past and Present*, edited by Andreas Exenberger and others (Innsbruck University Press, 2013), pp. 141–62; C. M. Peniston-Bird, *World Bibliographical Series: Vienna* (Santa Barbara, CA: ABC-Clio, 1997).

   5. Christopher Kennedy, *The Evolution of Great World Cities: Urban Wealth and Economic Growth* (University of Toronto Press, 2011).

   6. Greg Clark, *The Making of a World City: London 1991 to 2021* (Chichester: Wiley Blackwell, 2015).

## 5. Understanding Global Cities

   1. Peter Rimmer and Howard Dick, "The Historical Dimension," in *Global City Challenges: Debating a Concept, Improving the Practice*, edited by Michele Acuto and Wendy Steele (Basingstoke: Palgrave Macmillan, 2013), pp. 63–87.

   2. Chicago Department of City Planning, *Annual Report* (Chicago, 1911), p. 326.

   3. Delos Franklin Wilcox, *Great Cities in America: Their Problems and Their Government* (New York: Macmillan, 1913, pp. 182, 307.

   4. In Nicolas Beauduin and William Speth, *La vie des lettres* 3–4 (1913), p. 542.

   5. Patrick Geddes, *Cities in Evolution: An Introduction to the Town Planning Movement and to the Study of Civics* (London: Williams and Norgate, 1915), pp. 41–49.

   6. The Lloyd Mail, *Rotterdam Lloyd: Rotterdam* (1934), p. 72; "La patrie morave de Franz Schubert," in *L'Europe Centrale*, edited by Georges Marot, v. 13, nos. 1–26 (1938), p. 394.

   7. Jean Sibieude, *Tanger, ville internationale* (Paris: Librairie Coulet, Dubois et Poulain, 1927), p. 44. See also *L'Opinion* 12 (1919), p. 120.

   8. Paul Cohen-Portheim, *The Spirit of Paris* (London: B. T. Batsford, 1937), p. 106. Original published in German, *Paris* (Berlin: Klinkhardt und Biermann, 1930).

   9. Dartnell Corporation, "Sales Management," in *Survey of Buying Power* 52, nos. 1–13 (1943), p. 13.

10. Lewis Mumford, *The City in History: Its Origins, Its Transformations, and Its Prospects* (San Diego, Calif.: Harcourt, Brace and World, 1961), p. 561.

11. Neil Brenner and Roger Keil, "Editor's Introduction: Global City Theory in Retrospect and Prospect," in *The Global Cities Reader*, edited by Neil Brenner and Roger Keil (New York: Routledge, 2006), pp. 1–16.

12. Peter Hall, *The World Cities* (London: Weidenfeld and Nicolson, 1966).

13. Ibid., p. 7; Ferdinand Braudel, "Divisions of Space and Time in Europe," in *The Global Cities Reader*, edited by Brenner and Keil, pp. 25–31; Stephen Hymer, "The Multinational Corporation and the Law of Uneven Development," in *Economics and World Order from the 1970s to 1990s*, edited by J. Bhagwati (New York: Collier-Macmillan, 1972), pp. 113–40; D. A. Heenan, "Global Cities of Tomorrow," *Harvard Business Review* 55 (1977), pp. 79–92; Robert B. Cohen, "The New International Division of Labour, Multinational Corporations and Urban Hierarchy," in *The Global Cities Reader*, edited by Brenner and Keil, pp. 49–56; John Friedmann and Goetz Wolff, "World City Formation: An Agenda for Research and Action," *International Journal of Urban and Regional Research*, 6, no. 3 (1982) pp. 309–44.

14. Hymer, "The Multinational Corporation and the Law of Uneven Development," pp. 113–24.

15. David A. Heenan, "Global Cities of Tomorrow," *Harvard Business Review* 55 (May–June 1977).

16. Friedmann and Wolff, "World City Formation," p. 309.

17. R. G. Smith, "Beyond the Global City Concept and the Myth of 'Command and Control,'" *International Journal of Urban and Regional Research* 38, no. 1 (2014), pp. 98–115.

18. Doreen Massey, *World City* (Cambridge: Polity Press, 2007).

19. Peter J. Taylor and Ben Derudder, *World City Network: A Global Urban Analysis* (New York: Routledge, 2015).

20. Saskia Sassen, *The Global City: New York, London, Tokyo* (Princeton University Press, 1991).

21. London Planning and Advisory Committee, *London: World City Moving into the 21st Century* (London: HMSO, 1991).

22. Sassen, "Why Cities Matter," Venice Bienniale of Architecture Catalogue, (New York: Rizzolo, 2006), p. 27.

23. Mark Gottdiener, Leslie Budd, and Panu Lehtovuori, *Key Concepts in Urban Studies* (London: Sage, 2015); Michael Storper, *The Regional World: Territorial Development in a Global Economy* (New York: Guildford Press, 1997); Christof Parnreiter, "Global Cities in Global Commodity Chains: Exploring the Role of Mexico City in the Geography of Global Economic Governance," *Global Networks* 10, no. 1 (January 2010), pp. 35–53.

24. Jenny Robinson, *Ordinary Cities* (London: Routledge, 2006)

25. Gottdiener, Budd, and Lehtovuori, *Key Concepts in Urban Studies.*

26. Greg Clark and Tim Moonen, *Urban Innovation and Investment: The Role of International Financial Institutions and Development Banks* (London: Future Cities Catapult, 2014) (http://futurecities.catapult.org.uk/resource/urban-innovation -and-investment-full-report/).

27. These studies are reviewed in Clark, *The Making of a World City.*

28. Llewelyn Davies Planning and others, *Four World Cities: A Comparative Study of London, Paris, New York and Tokyo* (London: LDP, 1996). See also Peter Hall, "The Future Planning of City Regions," in *City Visions: Imagining Place, Enfranchising People,* edited by Mike Morrissey and Frank Gaffikin (London: Pluto Press, 1999), pp. 61–78; Les Budd and Michael Edwards, "Confirming Conforming Conventions: The Four World Cities Study," *City* 2, no.7 (1997), pp. 171–81.

29. OECD, *OECD Territorial Reviews: Competitive Cities in the Global Economy* (Paris: OECD, 2006), p. 17.

30. UN-Habitat, *The State of the World's Cities Report 2001* (Nairobi: UN-Habitat, 2001) (www.un.org/ga/Istanbul+5 /statereport1.htm); idem, *The State of the World's Cities: Prosperity of Cities* (Nairobi: UN-Habitat, 2012) (http://mirror.unhabitat.org /pmss/listItemDetails.aspx?publicationID=3387&AspxAuto DetectCookieSupport=1).

31. Richard C. Longworth, *On Global Cities* (Chicago: Chicago Council on Global Affairs, 2015), (https://www.the chicagocouncil.org/sites/default/files/On_Global_Cities.pdf).

32. A.T. Kearney, *Global Cities 2015: The Race Accelerates* (2015) (https://www.atkearney.com/documents/10192/5911137

/Global+Cities+201+-+The+Race+Accelerates.pdf/7b239156-86ac
-4bc6-8f30-048925997ac4); Joseph Parilla and others, *Global
Metro Monitor 2014: An Uncertain Recovery* (Brookings, 2015),
(www.brookings.edu/~/media/Research/Files/Reports/2015/01/22
-global-metro-monitor/bmpp_GMM_final.pdf?la=en).

33. Greg Clark and Tim Moonen, *World Cities and Nation
States* (Oxford: Wiley-Blackwell, 2016).

34. For example, UN-Habitat, *CPI Global City Report 2015*
(Nairobi: UN-Habitat, 2016) (http://unhabitat.org/cpi-global
-city-report-2015/).

6. *Global Cities Today*

1. GaWC, "The World According to GaWC 2012," 2013
(www.lboro.ac.uk/gawc/world2012t.html).

2. Richard Dobbs and others, *Urban World: The Shifting
Global Business Landscape* (New York: McKinsey Global Institute, 2013) (www.mckinsey.com/global-themes/urbanization
/urban-world-the-shifting-global-business-landscape).

3. See JLL Global Cities Research, "The Global 300 City
Toolkit," 2016 (www.jll.com/cities-research/Documents/cities
_research/Comparison/cities-microsite/bubble/Clustering
.html).

4. Korea Research Institute for Human Settlements, *Growth
Management of the Capital Region* (Seoul: Kyunghwan Kim,
2013).

5. Tom Symons, "What Can England's New Mayors Learn
from the Transformation of Seoul City Government?," NESTA,
December 2, 2015 (www.nesta.org.uk/blog/what-can-englands
-new-mayors-learn-transformation-seoul-city-government)

6. Ian Skeet, *OPEC: 25 years of Prices and Politics* (Cambridge University Press, 1988).

7. Ericsson, *Networked Society Index 2014* (Stockholm:
Ericsson, 2014) (www.ericsson.com/res/docs/2014/networked
-society-city-index-2014.pdf); Expatistan, "Expatistan Cost of
Living World Map," 2016 (www.expatistan.com/cost-of-living
/index).

8. Mori Memorial Foundation, *Global Power City Index
2015: Summary* (October 2015) (http://www.mori-m-foundation
.or.jp/pdf/GPCI2015_en.pdf).

*7. The Future of Global Cities: Challenges and Leadership Needs*

1. Richard Dobbs and others, *Urban World: The Global Consumers to Watch* (New York: McKinsey Global Institute, 2016) (www.mckinsey.com/global-themes/urbanization/urban -world-the-global-consumers-to-watch).

2. JLL, *Investment Intensity Index March 2016* (2016) (www.jll.com/news/273/jll-real-estate-investment-intensity-index -march-2016).

3. Parag Khanna, "A New Map for America," *New York Times*, April 15, 2016 (www.nytimes.com/2016/04/17/opinion /sunday/a-new-map-for-america.html?_r=0).

4. Parag Khanna, *Connectography: Mapping the Global Network Revolution* (London: Hachette UK, 2016).

5. World Bank, *Competitive Cities for Jobs and Growth: What, Who and How* (Washington, D.C.: World Bank, 2015) (www-wds.worldbank.org/external/default/WDSContentServer /WDSP/IB/2015/12/08/090224b083c371d5/2_0/Rendered/PDF /Competitive0ci000what00who00and0how.pdf); World Economic Forum, *The Competitiveness of Cities* (Geneva: World Economic Forum, 2014) (www3.weforum.org/docs/GAC/2014/WEF_GAC _CompetitivenessOfCities_Report_2014.pdf).

6. Parilla and others, *Global Metropolitan Monitor 2014*.

7. Tony Champion, Mike Coombes and Ian Gordon, "Urban Escalators and Inter-Regional Elevators: The Difference That Location, Mobility and Sectoral Specialisation Make to Occupational Progression," Discussion Paper 139 (London School of Economics, Spatial Economics Research Centre, 2013).

8. Enid Slack and André Côté, "Comparative Urban Governance," Future of Cities Working Paper (London: Foresight, U.K. Government Office for Science, July 2014), p. 12.

9. Rose Compans, "Metropolitan Ungovernability," *R. B. Estudos Urbanos e Regionais* 17, no. 2 (2015), pp. 11–24; Chris Aulich, Graham Sansom, and Peter McKinlay, "A Fresh Look at Municipal Consolidation in Australia," *Local Government Studies* 40, no. 1 (2013), pp. 1–20.

10. Allison Bramwell and David A. Wolfe, "Dimensions of Governance in the Megacity: Scale, Scope and Coalitions in Toronto," in *Governing Urban Economies: Innovation and Inclusion*

*in Canadian City Regions,* edited by Neil Bradford and Allison Bramwell (University of Toronto Press, 2014), pp. 58–87.

11. Marcel Boogers, "Pulling the Strings: An Analysis of Informal Local Power Structures in Three Dutch Cities," *Local Government Studies* 40, no. 3 (2014), pp. 339–55.

12. Clark and Moonen, *World Cities and Nation States.*

# INDEX